Pathfinder®Guides

Map Reading Skills

An introduction to map reading and basic navigation

Terry Marsh

Acknowledgements

My grateful thanks go to Dennis and Jan Kelsall for reading the manuscript at draft and proof stages, and for offering helpful advice.

Illustrations are reproduced by kind permission of: Garmin (Europe) Ltd www.garmin.co.uk; Harvey Maps; Tom Hutton (front cover); Terry Marsh; Sat Map; www.scalex.com/uk; Silva Sweden AB.

 This product includes mapping data licensed from Ordnance Survey® with the permission of the Controller of Her Majesty's Stationery Office. © Crown Copyright 2009. All rights reserved. Licence number 150002047. Ordnance Survey, the OS symbol and Pathfinder are registered trademarks and Explorer, Landranger and Outdoor Leisure are trademarks of the Ordnance Survey, the national mapping agency of Great Britain.

Text: Terry Marsh
Editorial: Ark Creative (UK) Ltd
Design: Ark Creative (UK) Ltd

© Crimson Publishing, a division of Crimson Business Ltd

ISBN: 978-0-7117-4978-8

While every care has been taken to check the accuracy and reliability of the information in this book, the author and publisher cannot accept responsibility for errors or omissions or for changes in details given. It is advisable to act with due care and attention, and follow basic safety rules, at all times when walking in the countryside, and to observe the law and the Countryside Code.

For more information visit the official website of the *Pathfinder*® and *Short Walks* guides: www.totalwalking.co.uk

First published 2007 by Jarrold Publishing, part of Pitkin Publishing. Reprinted 2008, 2009

This edition first published in Great Britain 2009 by Crimson Publishing, a division of:
Crimson Business Ltd,
Westminster House, Kew Road, Richmond, Surrey, TW9 2ND

Printed in Singapore. 3/09

A catalogue record for this book is available from the British library.

email: info@totalwalking.co.uk
www.totalwalking.co.uk

Contents

Discover the great outdoors with map-reading skills

Introduction

R eading maps is easy; you simply unfold them, put them the right way up, find what you're looking for on the map, and then plot your route or your location.

Except, of course, it isn't quite that simple. Some fortunate people can look at a map, understand what it's all about, and take to it instantly. The majority are not so blessed, and understanding and getting the most out of maps takes a little more effort. I was one of the lucky ones, but didn't realise it until, during the first of many years teaching about map reading and basic navigation at a local adult education centre, I suddenly realised that I didn't know how to explain the things I was doing instinctively. This induced panic, which gradually transformed into methodology and then a comprehensive set of notes that now form the foundation of this book.

But there really is no mystery to reading maps; it is all very logical because everything on a map means something.

And now is an excellent time to begin map reading because Ordnance Survey has recently completed a reorganisation of its maps for walkers, showing agreed areas of Access Land where you can explore freely; they use the latest technology in map production, and they are as up-to-date as can be. It's just a question of sitting down – and also getting out into the countryside – then working your way through the lines and dots and symbols stage by stage.

It is frustrating to enjoy walking in the countryside but to lack the confidence to read maps sufficiently well to be able to plot new routes or explore beyond the limits of walking guidebooks. This book will help you along the way, literally.

It is important to realise, however, that there are skills, not just of map reading, but of navigation, too, that lie beyond the scope of this book. Advanced navigation – what to do in white-out conditions, navigating using colleagues in a line ahead (leap frogging), navigating using the stars, and resection, for example – is a topic in its own right, for which the instructional 'bible' is *Mountaincraft and Leadership* by Eric Langmuir.

There is much more to staying safe on the British hills than basic navigational techniques. There are many considerations such as equipment, food and drink, weather, all of which, navigation too, take on a whole new dimension in winter conditions. *Map Reading Skills* is intended to get you started on the basics and to provide a foundation.

A brief history of mapping

'On 21 June 1791, a small entry was made in the Expense Ledger of the Board of Ordnance recording the payment of £373.14s, to Jesse Ramsden for a 3-foot theodolite. The purchase was made at the instigation of the Master General, the 3rd Duke of Richmond, and this insignificant entry is now generally accepted as the founding action of the Ordnance Survey.'

Tim Owen and Elaine Pilbeam
Ordnance Survey: Map Makers to Britain since 1791

As David Everett (1769–1813) wrote,
'Large streams from little fountains flow,
Tall oaks from little acorns grow',
and so it was with Ordnance Survey; they've been making maps of ever-increasing sophistication ever since. Today, they are the envy of the world.

The quality of mapping had been on the increase for centuries. The die had already been cast by Christopher Saxton (c.1543–c.1610) who was born in Yorkshire and as a young man gained an enthusiasm for and understanding of map-making.

In the time of Elizabeth I, William Cecil (later Lord Burghley) saw the importance of effective maps and as a result Saxton was commissioned to survey the whole of England and Wales, a mammoth task for the era. The survey began in the early 1570s, and by 1574 the first plates had been engraved. By 1577 the whole of England was completed with the survey of Wales being finalised the following year.

In the end, the resulting atlas comprised a general map of England and Wales together with 34 maps either of individual or grouped counties. The atlas set the standard both in accuracy and decorative detail – so much so that it remained the basis for succeeding county maps for more than 100 years.

By the 1790s, Britain still had no accurate national map, nor the survey material on which one could be based. Moreover, the Jacobite uprisings, culminating in the Battle of Culloden, highlighted the need for accurate military maps. It was from this that the production of maps steadily arose, leading by a complicated route to the establishment of the Ordnance Survey, as we know it today.

(The full story of the Ordnance Survey, for anyone who might want to study it further is detailed in the book by Owen and Pilbeam from which the opening quotation is taken.)

The trouble with maps

The first thing to realise about maps is that unlike the three-dimensional world in which we live, maps are printed on flat sheets of paper, and are therefore two-dimensional. This means that cartographers, those remarkably clever people who make maps, have to devise a means of showing three-dimensional information in a two-dimensional format. And in a way that is at least moderately intelligible.

The second oddity about maps is that while they are remarkably accurate, from another point of view they are incredibly inaccurate. This is partly because to make them manageable they have to be designed to a scale that crams a value-for-money amount of information onto a folded sheet of paper that doesn't require an estate car to carry it around. Something has to give; when you squeeze 20 kilometres' worth of information into less than one metre, it simply isn't possible to show every detail.

The way map-makers deal with this 'compression', getting a lot into a little, is by using a technique called 'scale'. Scale can be very confusing, but only if you think about it too much.

Understanding scale

Let's look at an illustration: I want to do a plan of my housing estate. It isn't a very big estate, probably just 100 metres in each direction. Now, I can get a piece of paper that is also 100 metres in each direction, and measure everything very, very accurately, and plot it all on my huge piece of paper. But then there isn't room in my house for such a massive plan, and there is a limit to how many times I can fold it – eight apparently.

No, what I want to do is put everything onto a piece of paper measuring just one metre in each direction. So, what I have to come up with is a system that allows me to take one unit of measurement of the actual estate, and substitute a much smaller unit of measurement to represent the larger unit. It doesn't matter what units I choose; I just have to be smart enough to come up with something that fits my one-metre square sheet of paper.

What I could do, for example, is to take one metre of the 'real' world, and show it on my piece of paper as one centimetre. One metre equals one centimetre; so 100 metres (the size of my estate) equals 100 centimetres, which fits neatly onto my piece of paper, which is 100 centimetres wide. What I've done is to use scale in order to make things fit.

That's all scale is. Making things fit.

So what scale is best for walking?

A map drawn to a large scale, i.e. my 'one metre equals one centimetre' map shows a lot of information. At the other extreme, a map on which one kilometre is represented by one centimetre, crams more 'distance' into the map, but contains much less detailed information. The latter would be good for motoring, the former, i.e. large-scale, is good for walking. A large-scale map will show rivers and streams fairly accurately along with field boundaries and individual buildings as well as other detailed features.

For many years the walker's 'map bible' was the Ordnance Survey *One-Inch* map (first created in 1801 for the area of Kent), on which one inch represented one statute mile. The scale, for the mathematically minded, was 1:63360, i.e. one unit of measurement (be it an inch or a foot, or whatever) on the map equated with 63,360 units of the same measurement on the ground. These early maps were a revelation, and much-prized by walkers. Even today, some of them are collectors' items. It took 190 maps to cover the whole of Britain.

When conversion to metric began, an adjustment to the scale was introduced. So, it became 1:50000, or 1¼ inches to 1 mile. With slightly more space on the map given to the same area as the older maps, these new maps were a great improvement, but were simply an enlarged version of the *One-Inch* maps. Eventually we were treated to new maps re-surveyed at the larger 1:50000 scale; these became what today are known as the *Landranger* maps. Two hundred and four maps were needed to cover the whole of Britain.

The reasons why these changes occurred is not vital; suffice to say, things became even better when maps appeared to a scale of 1:25000, or $2\frac{1}{2}$ inches to 1 mile. Today, Ordnance Survey maps at this scale are part of the *Explorer* series. The different scales are depicted in Figure 1.

Unlike the *One-Inch* and *Landranger* maps, when the *Explorer* map series was completed, a number of 'combined' or 'special' maps were produced that did not fit into the format of the standard maps, but which were specifically intended to meet the needs of visitors to popular destinations like the Lake District, the Yorkshire Dales, and so on. These special maps were called *Outdoor Leisure* maps, but they are essentially *Explorer* maps joined together to deal with particular areas.

If there is a problem with the Ordnance Survey *Explorer* and *Outdoor Leisure* maps it is simply that they are intended to serve a number of purposes, and are not exclusively for walkers. So, information appears on the maps, such as the location of craft centres, fishing areas, country parks and caravan sites, that is not vital to walking. Harvey Maps of Doune in Perthshire, however, who began by making maps for orienteering purposes, today produce maps dedicated to walking. Originally, they were at the unusual scale of 1:40000, and occasionally at 1:30000. But increasingly, Harvey Maps have covered most of the walking areas of Britain at a scale of 1:25000.

When you are familiar with maps at all scales, it becomes readily obvious that those at 1:25000 are by far the best for walking, and these are the maps ordinarily used in Crimson walking guides

Fig 1: Maps of The Lakes showing the same area at different scales

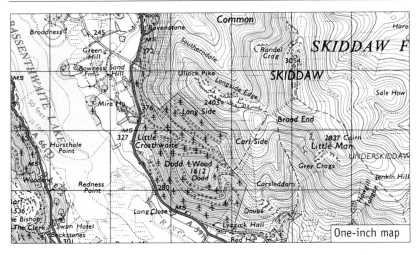

One-inch map

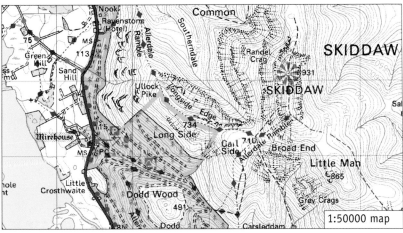

1:50000 map

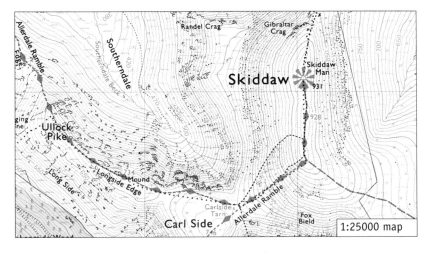

1:25000 map

(although occasionally slightly reduced in order to fit the pages).

Are there any problems with maps?

Well, yes, there are.

To begin with maps cannot be wholly accurate. In fact, it is probably safe to say that a map is in some way out-of-date the moment it is published. Changes are happening all the time and it is inordinately complex to keep track of them. Ordnance Survey has a mapping intelligence unit responsible for keeping track of all changes, and then feeding them through to the master maps. Even so, there are instances where, for example, field boundaries physically removed 40 years ago, still appear on maps. There is scope for improvement, as in all things, but realistically a modern Ordnance Survey map is as good as it gets.

Understanding 'North'

Some people have the uncanny knack of being able to spin round and face north; most of us just spin. In fact, it isn't a knack at all, it's a semi-conscious assimilation of basic information we are all aware of – the sun rises in the east and sets in the west and is roughly south at midday. If it's lunchtime, and you have your back to the sun (or where the sun would be if you could see it), then you are roughly facing north. Of course, we have the changes to accommodate 'summer time' to contend with. But as a rough guide, this system works … roughly.

This may seem like trivial information, but an awareness, even at a subliminal level, of where the sun is, and where it should be (approximately) in relation to your intended direction-of-travel, will often strike a note of confidence in your mind, or ring alarm bells. It's all part of the art of navigation, yet so many walkers fail to bring this little gem of knowledge into their repertoire of navigational skills.

So, where is north?

Without maps or compasses there would be only one 'North', that we commonly call the North Pole. When not otherwise qualified, the term **North Pole** usually refers to the **Geographic North Pole** – the northernmost point on the surface of the Earth, where the axis on which it spins intersects the Earth's surface. It's way up there in the middle of the frozen Arctic Ocean. For mapping purposes, this is called **True North,** and for walking needs, it can be disregarded – unless you're walking to the North Pole.

To make life difficult, there are a number of other 'Norths', two of which are important to map reading and navigation:

- **North Magnetic Pole** – the Earth's magnetic field is shaped roughly like that of a magnet and has two magnetic poles, one in the Canadian arctic, referred to as the North Magnetic Pole, and one off the coast of Antarctica, south of Australia, referred to as the South Magnetic Pole. At the North Magnetic Pole the Earth's magnetic field is directed vertically downward relative to the Earth's surface. North Magnetic Pole is the eventual destination for a walker who follows the compass needle from anywhere on Earth. Unfortunately, the North Magnetic Pole is constantly moving. Thankfully, the Geological Survey of Canada keeps track of this movement by periodically carrying out magnetic surveys to redetermine the pole's location. For the purposes of this book, the position of the North Magnetic Pole is called **Magnetic North.** Put simply, it's where your compass needle points.

> *Magnetic North is where your compass needle points.*

Fig 2: The position of the North Magnetic Pole in 2001

- **Grid North** – this is the direction of those vertical pale blue lines that, with those running east–west, form a grid on maps. Put simply, it's the top of the map.

Information about the relationship between true, grid and magnetic north is printed in the marginal data of maps as shown in Figure 3.

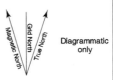

NORTH POINTS

At the centre of the N and S sheets true north is 0°42' east of grid north. Magnetic north is estimated at 3°00' and 2°58' west of grid north respectively for Jul 2007. Annual change is approximately 11' east

Magnetic data supplied by the British Geological Survey

Diagrammatic only

Fig 3: True, Grid and Magnetic North

If you compare the section on North Points in the marginal data of maps, you'll find that there are variations from map to map. This is not because the True North has changed but rather that the map represents a different part of the country, and so the angle to True North is different.

The horizontal angular difference between Grid North and Magnetic North is called **grid magnetic angle** or **magnetic variation**. This angle is particularly important when you come to using map and compass, and will be returned to in the chapter on 'Using Compasses'.

 Grid North is the top of the map.

Grid lines and grid references

Brief mention was made in the last chapter of that network of thin pale blue lines superimposed on maps. This is called the **National Grid.** The National Grid is a unique reference system that can be applied to the British Isles, using maps at any scale. Once you understand the grid, you can give your position, or identify the position of any feature, simply by using a short combination of letters and numbers; in fact, some people who live in remote countryside where street names and house numbers do not apply, often give their location as a grid reference. Youth hostels invariably do this. So, understanding grid references can mean the difference between finding a dry bed for the night, and not.

Knowing how to give and read grid references is vital in identifying the location of particular 'targets' you will visit – anyone using GPS systems (see 'GPS and other techniques') can plot these co-ordinates into their GPS receiver – and for giving your location to others. Grid references are a fundamental part of map reading, planning a walk and navigation. There is no mystique about them; they are logical, and easy to use, once they have been understood.

The National Grid

Imagine the whole of Britain covered by a grid of lines where the space between lines in each direction is 100 kilometres – see Figure 4 below.

In the diagram, each square is 100 kilometres in each direction, and is assigned two letters. There is nothing especially significant for walkers about these letters, but by using them as part of a grid reference it becomes possible to pinpoint (to within 100 kilometres), where a place is. The southern part of the Lake District, for example, is in square 'SD', the northern part in 'NY'; the most westerly part is in 'NX'. The legend on maps has a small diagram showing any overlap on the map between two or more lettered squares.

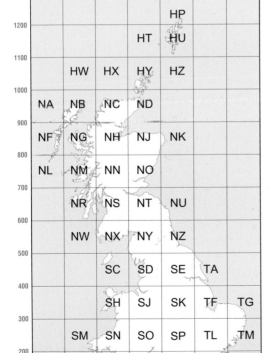

Fig 4: The National Grid

Grid references

The system of assigning letters to squares is the basis of what is known as a **grid reference**.

Of course, being accurate to only 100 kilometres is not good enough for walking. So, these 100-kilometre squares are further subdivided into smaller squares each representing 10 kilometres. In the following diagram, these 10-kilometre squares are numbered from 0–9 from the bottom left-hand (south-west) corner of the map moving in a left to right (easterly) direction, and from bottom to top (northerly) direction (see Figure 5).

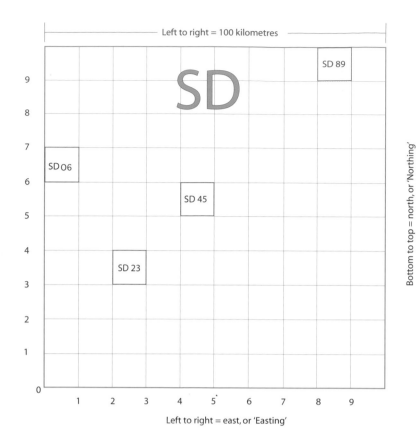

Fig 5: 100-kilometre grid square, showing 10-kilometre subdivisions

If you look closely at an Ordnance Survey *Explorer* map, along the bottom edge or the sides, at any point that is a multiple of 10, you'll notice that the pale blue lines are a little heavier than the rest. These are the boundaries of the 10-kilometre squares. Because *Explorer* (and other) maps cover areas larger than 10 square kilometres, there is more than one 10-kilometre square (or part of a square) on each map.

Using this system you can identify any 10-kilometre grid square, and arrive at a 10-kilometre square grid reference. In Figure 5, four have been identified – SD06, SD23, SD45 and SD89.

> The technique is to read first from left to right (called 'easting'), and then from bottom to top (called 'northing').

Once numbers come into the grid reference, the location starts to narrow down. The technique is to read first from left to right (this is called

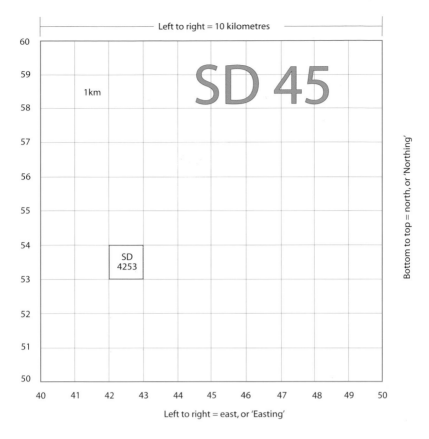

Fig 6: 10 kilometre grid square, showing 1-kilometre subdivisions

'EASTING'), and then from bottom to top (this is called 'NORTHING').

But this still isn't a sufficient degree of accuracy for walking. It will give a rough position of a feature, a lake, say, that overlaps one or more squares, but for walking, we need to zoom in a bit.

Let's look more closely at a 10-kilometre square: SD45. This is a 10-kilometre square, so, instead of using just '4' and '5', we must allow for the square to be further subdivided. So, we use '40' and '50'. It's the same square, we've just got closer to it – see Figure 6.

Now we can identify squares that are just one kilometre in each direction. In the example above, it is square SD 42 53. If you were on top of a hill on a clear day, you could see from one side of the square to the other. But by using this level of grid reference you could miss your destination by as much as one kilometre. So, we must zoom in another stage, to look more closely at square SD4253.

Once again, if you look at the margins of an *Explorer* map you will notice that between the grid numbers, each one-kilometre square is subdivided, but not numbered – 10 subdivisions in each direction, but only around the borders of the map. This time there are no blue lines on the map.

Each subdivision now represents just 100 metres, and at this level of accuracy we can arrive at what is called a **six-figure grid reference**, one that gives an accuracy that is adequate for walking purposes.

You can further subdivide: get down to an accuracy of ten metres; this gives an **eight-figure grid reference**, or even an accuracy of one metre, to give a **ten-figure grid reference**. But the reality is that we do not need that level of precision. A six-figure reference, giving an accuracy of ten metres, is generally good enough.

Fig 7: The full reference for the illustrated point is SD427537

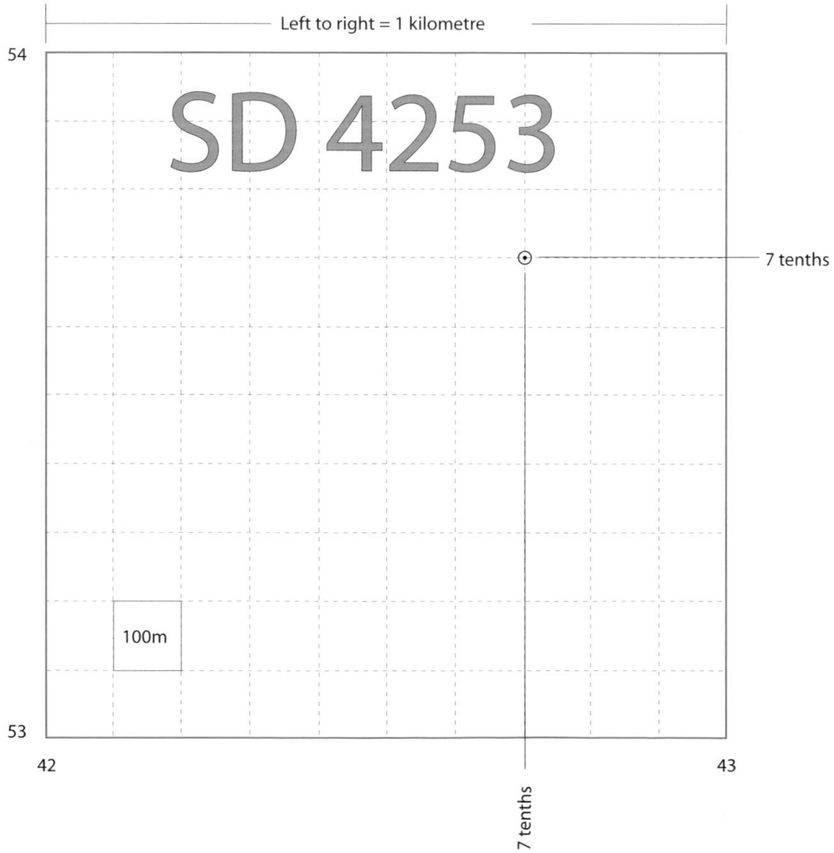

To arrive at a six-figure grid reference you begin by taking your grid letters (SD, in this example), then a two-figure reference (42), then a four-figure (4253), and finally estimate the one-tenth subdivisions of the 4253 square to arrive as closely as you can at the desired location – see Figure 7 – and remember to read **eastings** first (west to east/left to right) and then **northings** (south to north/bottom to top). In this example, the target easting is estimated to be seven-tenths of the distance left to right, and the northing also seven-tenths, but from bottom to top.

From this illustration, albeit it in an enlarged state, you can see that should you want greater precision, then you can continue subdividing the squares. But at the scale of maps used for walking, this level of accuracy is difficult to achieve. GPS receivers (about which there is more in the chapter 'GPS and other techniques') give a ten-figure grid reference, i.e. to an accuracy of 1m, but, because of the number of satellites and their positions, have an accuracy of only 5–10m at best, which rather makes a nonsense of a ten-figure reference.

In giving grid references in text, it is often useful to prefix everything with the letters 'GR', i.e. GR SD427537, to signify that the number is a

Fig 8: Extract from OS Explorer Sheet 296, showing location of grid reference SD427537: Cockersand Abbey

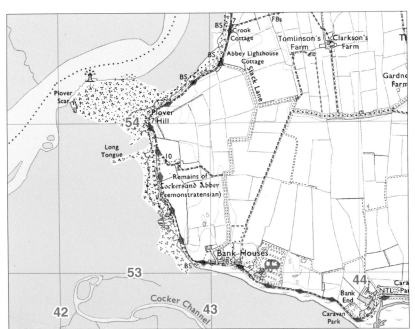

grid reference, but the way this appears in print differs from publisher to publisher, and is not vital.

For completeness, the map extract (Figure 8) and picture (Figure 9) show the grid reference we have been working towards: it's Cockersand Abbey near Lancaster.

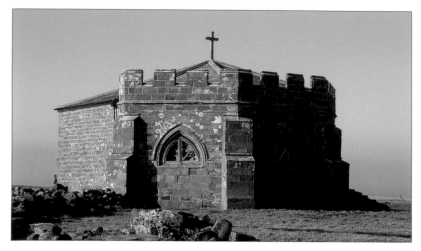

Fig 9: Having followed the grid referencing this far, here is what Cockersand Abbey looks like today

Back to the National Grid

Finally, because each National Grid square can be subdivided, it follows that the numbers 427537 will appear in each 100-kilometre square, i.e. at 100-kilometre intervals. This is the reason for using the two letters. But for every day use the letters can be omitted as the six-figure reference will not appear elsewhere on the map in your hand.

Understanding contours

Contours are wonderful: they tell you so much more about the terrain you're proposing to walk into than perhaps anything else on a map. Most importantly, they tell you whether the landscape is flat, undulating, hilly or too steep even to think about. But they are tricky little things, and need a bit of time to understand them properly.

Put simply, a **contour** is an imaginary line (they appear only on maps, sadly) that joins up all the points on the ground that are of the same height. What contours by themselves do not tell us is whether the land is going up or going down. To get this information, we need other clues: two in particular. One is the relationship between the contours – which are higher, which are lower. In other words, we need to know the height of the contours. The other big clue is rivers and streams, since, thanks to gravity, they flow downwards. Unfortunately, even in a wet country like Britain, there are a few places where there are no rivers and streams: then we have to rely on contours.

Contour intervals

Contours are shown on maps as reddish-brown lines spaced vertically at regular intervals. The marginal data on maps tells you what this interval is: it's called the **vertical interval.**

On maps to a scale of 1:25000, the vertical interval is usually five metres on lowland maps and ten metres on upland maps; on 1:50000 maps it is usually ten metres. Take a moment to check the interval on the map you are using. On some old maps of Ireland, the vertical interval was a massive 50 metres. A lot can happen in 50 metres, and the effect was to give the impression that all the hills in Ireland had flat tops. Of course they do not, but you need more refined vertical intervals to give a better idea of the shape of the land.

The height of contour lines

The height of contour lines is given on maps, but problems of space mean that not every contour line can be given a height. However, if you know the vertical interval you can easily count the lines from a numbered line and arrive at the correct height for any given contour. You just need to know whether you're counting up or down.

The horizontal spacing of contours is variable depending on the nature of the landscape. Flat terrain will have the contours spaced widely apart; steep terrain will have them close together.

> The height of contour lines is printed so that the top of the number points uphill.

To make life a little easier, **every fifth contour line is darker** and stronger than the others. What isn't instantly obvious, until you study maps a little more, is that the height of contour lines is always printed so that the top of the number is pointing uphill.

Interpreting contours

There are few places in Britain that are totally devoid of some form of man-made feature (see 'Landscape features'), but they may be widely spread, or obscured by dips in the landscape or by mist. So, the ability to read contours is, as the next illustration shows, vital.

Take a look at Figure 10 – it's actually of Great Mell Fell in the Lake District. Without the contour heights, while you might imagine that this is a hill, you could equally be looking into a chasm.

Moreover, this diagram also serves to illustrate that the closer the contour lines are in a horizontal relationship, the steeper the terrain.

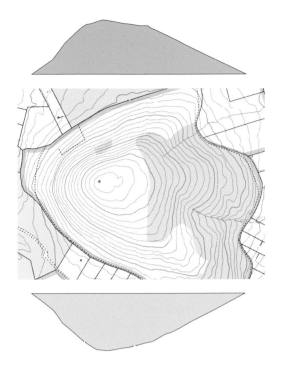

Fig 10: Is it a hill or a hole?

Now consider Figure 11. This shows three samples of contour line grouping. In all cases, the contour lines descend from left to right (for illustration purposes only).

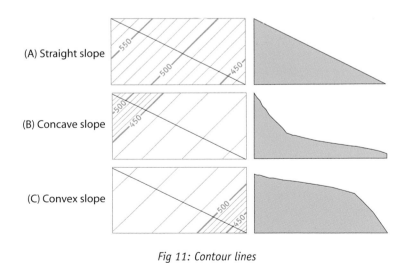

Fig 11: Contour lines

Where the contours are evenly spaced, then the slope is **uniform** (A). In (B) the contour lines are closer together on the left, and this denotes what is called a **concave** slope. Example (C) shows the contours more closely grouped on the right; this illustrates a **convex** slope.

Of course, things are not so simple in reality, and hill slopes are often a mix of all three types. Having an understanding of these three basic slope types, as depicted by contours on a map, will help when it comes to planning a walk, and in navigation. Relating the map to the ground is something dealt with in 'Reading and interpreting maps', but it is all based on being able to make the connection between the arrangement of contours and the actual landscape.

The togetherness of contours

The closer contours are grouped, as illustrated in Figure 11, the steeper the ground. This enables you to plan routes that, so far as possible, avoid steep ascents or descents. Understanding contours enables decisions to be made about choice of routes when dealing with terrain where rights of way are not present.

Spot heights

Dotted all over maps are small numbers. These are **spot heights**, i.e. heights that have been surveyed to the nearest metre above mean sea level. There are two types. Those shown in black are 'ground survey' heights; those in brown are 'air survey' heights. As a rule, up to 80 per cent of ground detail is collected using aerial photography, but this is not always possible because shadows, clouds, tree cover and overhanging eaves on buildings mean that the surveyor still has to carry out surveys on the ground.

> *Spot heights seen on maps are not visible on the ground.*

Heights shown close by a trig pillar (about which more in 'Landscape features') refer to the ground level height at the pillar, and do not necessarily refer to the height of a mountain or hill summit. Trig pillars are often on the summit of hills, but that is not their reason for being there, and the need to use them to make accurate surveys means that they are positioned where it is most convenient for surveys to be carried out.

One key thing to remember is that while trig pillars are visible, spot heights are not, and no reliance should be placed on them for detailed navigation. You will not find a spot height on the ground.

Access: roads, tracks, footpaths, bridleways and Access Land

For the purposes of this chapter reference is made mainly to Ordnance Survey *Explorer* maps and the information they contain. This information is represented in slightly differing ways and colours on other maps, but is essentially the same.

As explained earlier, a map is simply a representation on paper of an area of terrain, a bird's-eye view, in fact. But unlike a bird's-eye view or aerial photograph, which shows everything visible, a map is selective. Map-makers choose what information to put on a map, notably those objects likely to be of interest to the people for whom the map is intended, like paths, roads, streams, rivers and bridges. These are represented diagrammatically: a barn is not depicted with a sloping roof, nor necessarily at a precise size – on small-scale maps this simply isn't possible – but by means of a small rectangle. The *position* of features on maps is likely to be remarkably accurate, but in terms of relative size, they may be exaggerated – roads and foot-paths, for example, are wider on a scale map than they are in real life. This technique is a kind of shorthand used by cartographers. But so that you understand the keys that the map-maker is using, all this information, about paths and buildings, roads and streams is

---

annotated somewhere on the map, generally in one large panel at the side of the map. It's worth spending time studying this, and, first, identifying the features and the shorthand symbols for them that you are most likely to need: if you are walking in the Yorkshire Dales, it's unlikely you'll need to know the difference between an operational lighthouse and a non-operational one. But walk along the coast of Britain, and a lighthouse might be significant in plotting your desired location.

So, let's take a look at the most directly relevant symbols that you'll need to recognise and understand; we can return to the others later. The following are all taken from the *Explorer* series of maps.

Roads and tracks

Other than motorways, you can walk on roads. They are open to all traffic. Busy main roads, however, are not fun to walk along, although it may be necessary to include them in a walk for short stretches. But many of the minor roads are a delight to walk, and make for speedy (or unhurried, leisurely) progress.

To make life easy, the different classes of roads are colour-coded on maps (see Figure 12).

Fig 12: Roads and tracks as depicted on Ordnance Survey maps

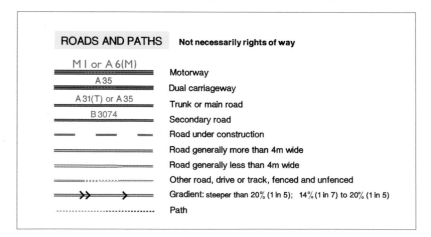

Motorways are shown in blue; main roads in red. Secondary roads, the B-roads, are brown. The map legend even differentiates between roads over or under four metres in width. Those less than four metres wide are depicted in yellow, and these are the roads most usually found in rural locations. Look closely at the map, however, and you may pick out that while most roads have a solid line on both sides of them, some do not, or have a dotted line. A solid line tells you that the road is either fenced or has a wall beside it (on one or both sides); a dotted line signifies that the road is unenclosed. These are customarily found across common land or open upland pastures to which there is a traditional and long-standing right of free access.

Fig 13: Walled 'white road' – an 'Occupation' road – across Twiston Moor, Pendle

Roads in housing estates are invariably shown as white but out in the countryside there are other so-called **'white roads'** (see Figure 13 above). These can be anything from a surfaced lane to a private drive; maybe they depict the course of an old 'green lane' or an ancient packhorse route. Sometimes they may be what are known as 'Occupation' roads, i.e. service tracks for the flanking landowners, along which they drive sheep or cattle and farm vehicles. These are splendid to walk, but whether you can do so legally is not information found on maps. That's a pity because they often connect other, legitimate, routes, and have a sense of history about them.

So, how do you find out? With some, the position is clear. If you encounter a white road with green dots along it, then the road is an 'unclassified county road', which you can walk along. All others are private. Often, walkers are tolerated along these; many are centuries' old thoroughfares. But the only sure way to find out is when you arrive on one: if there is a 'Private' sign, then you need an alternative route to switch to. You may get away with walking white roads, but that's all you are doing – getting away with it: you cannot be certain that you are walking the route lawfully.

Footpaths and bridleways

Until what has become known as 'Access Land' was created in England and Wales under the *Countryside and Rights of Way Act 2000 (CROW)*, when you walked in the countryside you were confined to using public **rights of way**, many of which have their roots in long-established pedestrian (and other) routes across the countryside.

The situation was slightly different in Scotland. Walkers in Scotland have long enjoyed a moral and de facto right of access. Nothing much has changed except that this is now enshrined in *The Land Reform (Scotland) Act 2003*. The Act tells you where you have right of access and *The Scottish Outdoor Access Code* sets out your responsibilities when exercising your rights. These rights came into effect in February 2005.

> There is a point of view that rights of way provide freedom of access to the countryside; there is another view that they are actually restrictions on freedom because walkers are confined to the course of the path.

Footpaths on maps are denoted by a black dotted line (see Figure 14), but they are simply that – a footpath, and not necessarily a lawful right of way. Where rights of way exist along a footpath, they are shown on Ordnance Survey *Explorer* maps in green, and are properly described as 'Public footpaths'. In Scotland, where the rights of way system is different and less developed than in England and Wales, public footpaths and

Fig 14: Footpath, bridleway, BOATs and RUPPs as depicted on Ordnance Survey maps

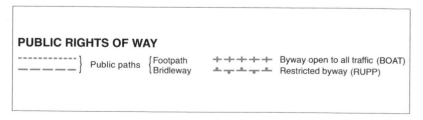

PUBLIC RIGHTS OF WAY

‑‑‑‑‑‑‑‑‑‑‑‑‑ } Public paths { Footpath ┼ ┼ ┼ ┼ ┼ Byway open to all traffic (BOAT)
— — — — — { Bridleway ┴ ┬ ┴ ┬ ┴ Restricted byway (RUPP)

bridleways are not shown in green, but are depicted as a black dashed line instead.

The terms 'public right of way' and 'highway' both mean a way over which the public have a right to pass and re-pass. There is a distinction, however, in that a 'right' is an abstract thing, while a 'highway' is in essence a strip of land. The nature of the right determines the type of way, which can be either:

- a **footpath** (marked on maps by small green dashes) over which the right of way is on foot only; or

- a **bridleway** (marked by larger green dashes) over which the right of way is on foot and on horseback.

In 1968, Parliament granted cyclists the right to use bridleways, and also introduced the notion of **cycle tracks** (see page 33) over which there is a right to cycle, and possibly also to walk.

In addition to footpaths and bridleways, which are the principal routes for the enjoyment of walking, there are two other categories depicted on Ordnance Survey maps:

- **Byway Open to All Traffic** (BOAT): this is a special category (shown on maps as a line of small green elongated crosses). BOATs are technically carriageways, and so a right of way for vehicular traffic, but used mainly for the purposes for which footpaths and bridleways are used, namely, by walkers and horse-riders.

- **Road Used as a Public Path** (RUPP): which is exactly what it is (shown on maps as a line of alternating flattened green 'T's). RUPPs are 'restricted byways' over which the public has a right of way for vehicles other than mechanically propelled vehicles, so giving a right of way on foot, on horseback or leading a horse, and for cyclists.

Figure 15 shows the relative incidence of each of the above rights of way in England.

Most of the rights of way encountered on a walk are either public footpaths or bridleways, but while maps depict them, there is no guarantee that they actually exist on the ground. Many will have become overgrown or blocked, and there is really only one way to find out – you have to walk them, and be prepared to make changes.

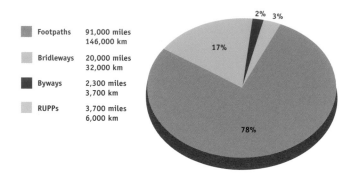

Composition of the national network

■ Footpaths	91,000 miles	146,000 km
░ Bridleways	20,000 miles	32,000 km
■ Byways	2,300 miles	3,700 km
▒ RUPPs	3,700 miles	6,000 km

2% 3%

17%

78%

Fig 15: The national network of rights of way

Other routes with public access

In addition to the green-coloured rights of way, you find other symbols and colours that show where you may walk, but the exact nature in law, and any restrictions that apply to them, is often variable.

● **Permissive or concessionary paths and bridleways** (depicted in orange) are not rights of way, but show the course of routes for public use where the path has been negotiated with the landowner, but with the intention that they should never become rights of way. Because they are permissive, they can be closed, and the landowner may erect notices to that effect and, indeed, close them on at least one day a year to ensure that the public does not acquire a right of way. In practice, permissive routes provide missing links in the path network, and often lead to places of special interest or outstanding viewpoints.

● **National trails and long-distance routes** (depicted by green diamond-shaped lozenges) are recreational routes. Usually they follow existing rights of way, and the diamond symbol serves simply to mark the line of the route. Occasionally, however, they are not over defined rights of way, but along routes where permission to walk already exists, or is given. In such cases, the alignment shown on maps is no more than the best information available, and may have on-the-ground variations. You should use common sense when dealing with them, and observe any diversion signs.

● **Other routes** (depicted by a line of green dots) are usually found overlying white roads. They are a clear indication that you can use a white road for walking. The same symbol, but in orange, denotes a **traffic-free cycle route**; you can walk these, too. The expression **cycle track** has various meanings. In one sense, it can mean a way over which cyclists have a legal right of passage along with other users, such as bridleways. It can also mean a way over which cyclists can pass, usually along with others, by permission of the landowner – certain sections of the routes promoted by SUSTRANS (a charity promoting sustainable transport), and the Monsal Trail in the Peak District, fall into this category. In some areas, the expression means a way over which cyclists have exclusive right of passage. It can also be used to describe a public footpath that has been converted to a cycle track under the provisions of the *Cycle Tracks Act 1984*.

Access Land

Walking on Access Land provides the chance to explore huge areas of the countryside without resorting to paths of any kind or rights of way. Commonly known as the 'Right to Roam', this right covers some of the most wild and dramatic landscapes, heaths, moors, down and areas of registered common land. 'Access Land' is depicted on Ordnance Survey maps by a pale orange/brown tint, surrounded by a stronger orange/brown line. Access Land in woodlands is shaded green, as in Figure 16.

Fig 16: Example of boundaries of Access Land, and the distinctive shading used for Access Land in woodlands. Notice the different types of woodland shown on this extract

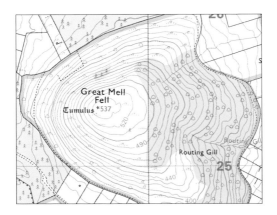

Within Access Land you can wander at will; whether you would want to is another matter. Often Access Land is truly wild and rough countryside, and anyone out for a gentle stroll with children will want to stick to established paths. True 'free roaming' is for strong walkers, and generally involves arduous terrain and rugged going, often without identifying features.

Small symbols – a letter 'i' within a red circle – show access points, where you can glean information about the extent of access land, any  restrictions that may apply, and actual points of ingress and egress to the land.

Landscape features: natural and man-made

One of the joys of walking in Britain is the exhilaration of striding out over wild, uncultivated moorland. It is one of the freedoms for which campaigners fought in the late 19th century – the struggle for access onto the moors around Bolton in 1896 – and almost 40 years later (1932) the more widely renowned trespass on Kinder Scout. For many years, when walkers enjoyed the open moors it was along existing public rights of way; all that changed when the provisions of the *Countryside and Rights of Way Act 2000 (CROW)* came into force. Under the Act, the public may walk freely on mapped areas of mountain, moor, heath, down and registered land without the need to stick to paths.

The new rights came into effect across the whole of England on 31 October 2005.

Understanding of rights of way, permissive paths and Access Land does not, however, provide enough information to enable you to plan a successful walk. Nothing so far mentioned says anything about the 'lie of the land'. Being able to recognise the many and varied landscape features will enable you to plot an enjoyable route.

There is a huge amount of information on a map, yet few newcomers to map reading take the time to study the detail. As a result, they fail to comprehend what the map is telling them, and how this information can be used to help with route planning and with navigation.

 Take time to study the map.

Natural features

Vegetation

Large expanses of sheep-cropped turf are a delight to walk but there are other types of vegetation which can make progress a less agreeable experience. Equally, bluebell-filled woodlands in springtime are a delight, except that the maps do not tell you about the bluebells, just the woodland.

The marginal data on maps shows the types of vegetation that can be found, distinguishing between coniferous and non-coniferous trees, coppiced woodland and orchards. Scrub, heath, saltings, reed beds, rough grassland and bracken are also depicted on maps, and give you some idea of the sort of terrain likely to be encountered.

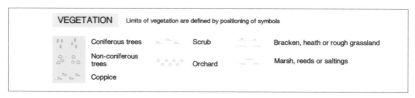

Fig 17: Vegetation types as shown on Ordnance Survey maps

What the maps cannot show is the condition or density of the vegetation. Coniferous plantations are often dark, tightly packed, gloomy and impassable; oak and beech woodlands are not – oak and beech just won't grow so closely together. So, you might want to avoid coniferous plantations, but be happy enough to tackle a route through an oak woodland. Notice that distinction between 'plantation' and 'woodland' – see Figure 17 above: the former is generally used to signify a commercial planting of trees, whereas a 'woodland', while possibly also planted, is likely to be more natural and pleasurable, and often truly native. Where the two occur, often broad-leaved trees and larch, for example, this is referred to as 'mixed woodland'.

For anyone following a route across country, woodlands and plantations are valuable aids to navigation. They have fairly regular and uniform boundaries, sometimes fenced, sometimes unfenced (as with roads), no two woodlands have the same shape, and they enable you to pinpoint exactly your position on the map.

Of course woodlands, and more frequently, plantations are felled and cleared; sometimes new ones are planted. But thankfully the rate of this activity is slow enough for it to have little serious impact on the accuracy of a map; even with a recently cleared plantation, you can see where it has been for many years afterwards.

Increasingly in recent years, many plantations have been made available for recreational use, and waymarked routes provided through them. But without waymarking and with the limited visibility that prevails in established plantations, it is easy to become disorientated. Moreover, it is difficult for narrow pathways through dense woodland to be plotted accurately on maps, and such conditions can often confuse even the most experienced map reader.

Rivers and streams

Depicted by blue lines with a thickness that roughly approximates to their width, rivers and streams feature on every one of the *Explorer* series of maps. Crossing points are usually shown either as a footbridge (FB), a 'Ford' or as 'Stepping Stones'. But it is not safe to assume that simply because a footpath runs down to a stream and continues on the other side there is necessarily a 'dry' crossing point. Fords can be of varying depth, and sometimes impassable. Nor are stepping stones wholly reliable. Often they may be under water, and seldom is it that they are uniformly flat, allowing walkers to step easily across. Quite frequently one or more of the stones becomes dislodged, leaving you with an uncomfortable step or jump to complete the crossing.

If you look closely at a 1:25000 map you can see if the green footpath line has solid black lines on both sides. In this case, there is likely to be some secure form of crossing but otherwise, it can be a guessing game with a damp answer.

Lakes and reservoirs

Water is depicted on maps in pale blue surrounded by a deep blue line. It is quite obvious which areas are lakes, but a little less obvious which are reservoirs. The give-away with reservoirs, although not always so, is a straight edge to the 'lake' where the dam has been formed. Many lakes and reservoirs are now open to walkers, and provide a key focal point to enjoyment of the countryside.

Crags, loose rock, boulders, outcrop and scree

These various forms of landscape feature will almost certainly have an influence on route planning, and need to be recognised. There are differing symbols for each (see Figure 18), but all should be thought of at best as arduous and dangerous terrain, and at worst a 'no go' zone ideally to be avoided. Many parts of Britain are, however, craggy, and, for many, desirable places to be.

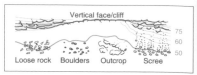

The symbols for crags, loose rock, boulders, outcrop and scree should be regarded as a warning that, combined with other map symbols and

Fig 18: Symbols for crags, loose rock, boulders, outcrop and scree as depicted on Ordnance Survey maps

information, determine whether it is somewhere safe to walk.

Man-made features

Field boundaries

Maps are draped with thousands of field boundaries, shown as thin black lines. What the map cannot show is whether the boundary is a wall, fence or a hedgerow, or what size the wall, hedge or fence is.

Maps do not indicate how such boundaries might be crossed. If a footpath is indicated crossing a field boundary, there will be some form of crossing point – one of the numerous forms of stile, as a rule, but not all of them are accommodating of persons of generous girth (see Figure 19 below).

Fig 19: Boundaries and stiles can vary greatly on the ground

Grubbed out field boundary alongside old green track

Stone gap stile – a tight squeeze

As land use changes, so field boundaries disappear, but it is often a long time before they disappear from maps. There are instances of field boundaries shown on maps that were physically removed more than 40 years ago. From a practical point of view all that this does is generate the need to be aware that field boundaries may have gone. It is an easy thing to become confused if an expected (and depicted) field boundary is no longer there on the ground. But an awareness that this sort of thing happens will reassure you; quite often you can still see where the original boundary lay.

In spite of these inherent difficulties, field boundaries are one of the surest forms of navigation. There are few boundaries that are straight, and these in-built bends and sudden changes of direction are a great help in both determining where exactly you are, and in spotting the boundaries that are missing.

Triangulation pillars

Popularly known as 'trig' pillars, these obelisks of surveying days of old are a part of British heritage, much loved especially by walkers who may be temporarily misplaced in their travels and then suddenly find one, and, above all else, a clear and precise indication of an exact location. All trig pillars have been very accurately surveyed, and Ordnance Survey archives contain details of their position and height to many decimal places. In poor visibility, they are crucial. On maps they are identified by a small blue triangle with a dot at its centre.

Fig 20: In winter conditions, on bleak moorland, isn't it good to know exactly where you are? This is a trig pillar at Gragareth – the highest summit in Lancashire

These days the Ordnance Survey uses satellites to fix positions, making the familiar trig pillars obsolete. But they have been around for many years, and it will be a long time before they disappear from our landscape, if at all. Each one carries a specific identifying number in a brass plate near its base. Walkers have been known to annotate maps with the identification number of trig pillars visited; if nothing else, it proves you were there.

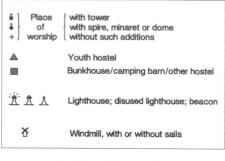

Fig 21: Building symbols

Buildings

Generally, buildings are shown on maps as small rectangles that approximate, as near as they reasonably can, to the size and shape of the real thing. They are almost invariably in exactly the correct position, i.e. they are not randomly placed onto the map. So, you can rely on them for navigational purposes.

Farm buildings and field barns are the most common buildings represented by a rectangle. But if you look at the legend on the map border you will see that some buildings have very specific symbols – churches, other places of worship, youth hostels, bunkhouses, camping barns, lighthouses and windmills.

All are very useful, but among these, three symbols are especially effective in helping to find your way when out on a walk. These are the symbols for places of worship, and there are three kinds:

- A **church with a tower** is shown in black as a small cross on top of a square. Think of the square as a squat tower, and you'll never be confused.

- A **church with a steeple** is shown in black as a small cross on top of a circle. The 'think square, think tower' suggestion does not work with steeples. But, if it's not a tower, it must be a steeple.

- A **chapel** or a church with neither a tower nor a steeple is shown in black as a small cross.

As long established features of our British countryside, churches are wonderful navigational aids. Not only do they confirm where you are or that you are heading in the right direction if you see them in the distance, but if your map says you should be heading towards a church with a tower and you can see a church with a steeple up ahead, you know something is wrong, and can check before you walk too far off-route.

There is another interesting point about churches that can help with orientation. Most (but not all) churches are built on an east-west alignment, usually with the tower or steeple at the western end.

Distance and heights

C alculating distance by using a map is not an exact science. Nor can it be. Given that a map is a scaled-down view of things, it follows that the level of accuracy, when measuring distances, is limited. But it rarely matters that in a walk of, say 10km, you need to be accurate to a few metres. What you may need to know is whether the distance you have to walk is 9 kilometres, 10 kilometres or 11 kilometres, because this will affect how long it will take you to do the walk (see 'How long will it take?' in 'Planning a walk').

Rough and ready

What makes measuring distance really easy is that the map is already conveniently overlain with a measuring device – the grid, and each square represents one kilometre. Take a look at the map extract (Figure 22) on the next page.

With such a ready guide, it is comparatively easy to roughly measure distance. Allowing for the various kinks and bends in the route, but using the one-kilometre grid as a guide, you can roughly calculate the walk to be around 9km (the guidebook gives 8km). In fact, when measured accurately, the walk is 8.93km. So, the rough calculation was easily good enough.

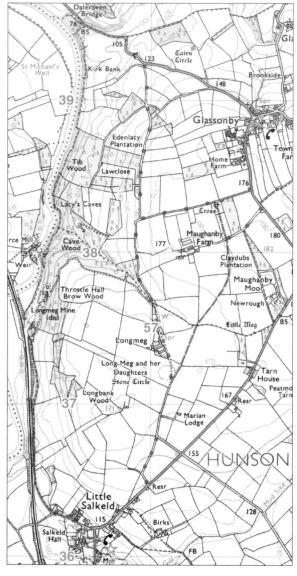

Fig 22: Little Salkeld, near Penrith, Cumbria

Once you get used to this technique, you become more adept at making these rough calculations. And the beauty is, it works at any scale. Just use the grid squares as a guide. This simple technique isn't scientifically accurate, but neither is it disastrously inaccurate. Rough measuring like this can be critical should you need to vary a route mid-walk in an emergency or for other reasons.

How long is a piece of string?

A remarkably accurate and inexpensive (but very fiddly) system to measure distance on a map, is to use a piece of string. Just ordinary parcel string, or a length of cotton thread will do. Lay the map flat on a table, place one end of the string at the start of the walk, and then simply tease the string along the route, feeding it out as you go, and taking care not to 'drag' it. When you get to the end, cut the string, and then measure it against a ruler, allowing 4cm for every kilometre for maps at 1:25000, and 2cm for

> To roughly convert kilometres to miles, multiply by 0.6, then round up. 16 kilometres x 0.6 = 9.6 miles, near enough.

1km for maps at 1:50000. Some suggest that you mark the string beforehand at 4cm or 2cm intervals, but this isn't necessary.

Map wheels

As an alternative to a length of string you could buy a map wheel (see Figure 23). This is useful for measuring when accuracy is especially important. Map wheels are calibrated to function at a number of scales, and work by measuring off distance as you wheel the device across your intended route on the map.

If you are using a scale that is not present on your map wheel, simply place the instrument back on the map, on a grid line, and run it back along the grid line until the instrument or its pointer reaches zero. Make a note of where on the map you reach zero, and then simply count the number of grid lines crossed; this gives the route distance in kilometres.

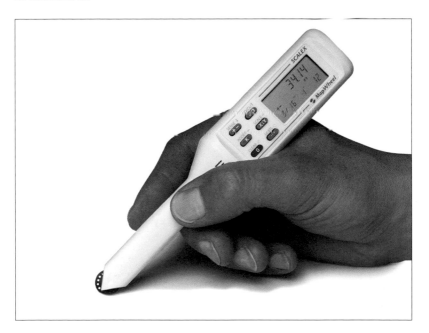

Fig 23: Modern map wheel

Romers

Of course, it does not take a lot of ingenuity to make a simple measuring device of your own, called a romer, by sticking an adhesive label to a ruler, and marking it up yourself, using the map edge as a guide.

You will find a romer around the edge of most compasses anyway (see 'Introducing the compass').

A word of caution

There is another relatively minor issue concerning the measurement of distance to introduce at this stage. In fact, there are two variations on the same issue.

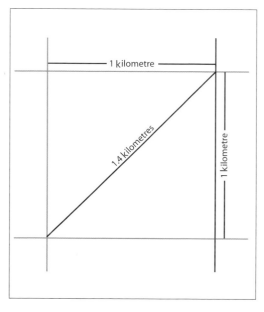

First, if you are using the one kilometre grid square to measure distance, you need to understand that it only measures one kilometre horizontally and vertically. Those adept at geometry will instantly understand, but take a look at the illustration (Figure 24).

It's simple Pythagoras. It just means that the distance across the diagonal is 40 per cent more than horizontally or vertically.

Fig 24: Kilometre grid square

Second, if you measure a distance of one kilometre on a map, then, if the land is flat, one kilometre is the actual distance you have to travel. On the other hand, if the kilometre is across steep or undulating terrain, then the distance is going to be a little farther.

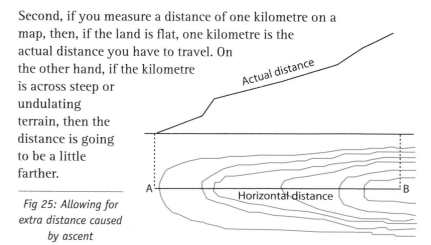

Fig 25: Allowing for extra distance caused by ascent

If the ground is flat then the distance between A and B will be as measured. But if the ground is steep, as in Figure 25, then the distance from A to B will be longer. On a short walk the difference will be negligible; you just need to be aware of it. If A to B is 3,000 metres, and the height difference 400 metres, then the actual distance walked is 3,026.5 metres. But repeat that over a much longer walk, and you can see that the 'invisible' extra distance can amount to something to be reckoned with.

This neatly leads into calculating height, rather than distance.

Calculating height

To find the height of a feature by looking at the map, you need to find the nearest contour line to it that has a value, or use a nearby spot height (see page 26) if there is one. If you are using a spot height, remember that the given height is of the spot and not a contour line.

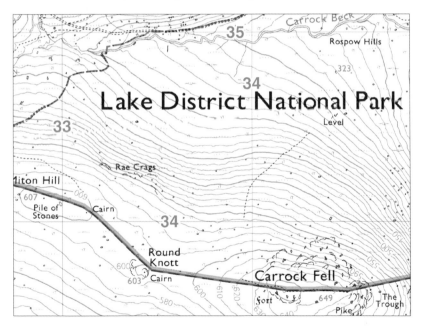

Fig 26: Extract from Outdoor Leisure Map 5

Consider Figure 26 above, and imagine that you want to calculate the height of Rae Crags (GR 334343). The crags are on a bold line, but the line does not have a contour height number. The nearest number is 600 metres; the top of the number points up hill, remember. So, Rae Crags are lower than 600 metres.

The extract in Figure 26 is from a 1:25000 map, and the contour interval on upland maps is 10 metres. Count the number of contour lines down to Rae Crags: five. Multiply by the contour interval, 10 metres (50 metres), and subtract from 600, to put Rae Crags on the 550-metre contour line.

If you want to check that you've done this correctly, there is another spot height (323) near GR 345348. The interval between the bold contour lines is 50 metres, so count down from the 600-metre contour. The bold contour line just above the spot height is 350 metres, and the spot height between two and three single contour lines lower down, i.e. between 330 metres and 320 metres. Of course, you could just as easily have used the spot height, 323, to count up to Rae Crags.

The nature of the landscape often means that contour heights cannot always be given uniformly across the map, so you do need to recognise that sometimes you'll be counting up to a height, and sometimes down.

Calculating height difference

Height difference is just that: the difference between two heights. Go back to Figure 26. The height difference between spot height 323 and Rae Crags (550 metres) is simple subtraction – 227 metres.

But what is the height difference between spot height 323 and the summit of Carrock Fell? The danger here is that you are lulled by spot height 649, near the top of Carrock Fell, into thinking that marks the summit of the fell. But look more closely. The actual numbers 649 sit on the 640 metre contour line (the dot that is the spot height point is difficult to make out) and there is a bold contour line above that. This is 650 metres. And if you look even more closely you'll find a tiny circular contour line above that, which must be 660 metres. So, the top of Carrock Fell must be higher than 660 metres, and not 649 metres as the spot height might tempt you into thinking. The actual height is 661 metres, but you cannot see that on 1:25000 maps because the bit of Carrock Fell that reaches up to 661 metres is too tiny to figure on maps at that scale.

So, the height difference between spot height 323 and the top of Carrock Fell using the information from the 1:25000 map is 337+ metres, but in fact 338 metres if you know the correct height for Carrock Fell (it is given on the 1:50000 Ordnance Survey *Landranger* Sheet 90).

Calculating height difference in this way is straightforward, but all it does is tell you just that, the difference between two heights. If the two heights are separated by a continually rising slope then the height difference is the amount of climbing you will have to do. But it is not necessarily the same as the amount of height you would have to climb on a walk with numerous ups and downs.

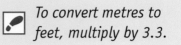

To convert metres to feet, multiply by 3.3.

Calculating height gain goes one step further.

Calculating height gain

Height gain is the amount of height you have to climb on a walk, and is the sum total of all the up sections, not just the difference between the starting point and the top of the mountain. Conversely, height loss is the sum of all the down sections. Figure 27 illustrates the point.

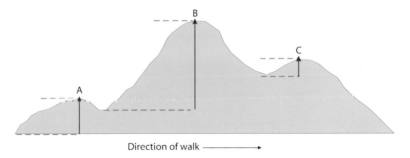

Direction of walk ———→

Fig 27: Height gain is the sum of the height difference at each of the three points A, B and C

Now look at Figure 28, and let's assume you want to calculate the height gain involved in walking from High Pike to Carrock Fell along the route marked.

The first thing to recognise is that there are certain known heights – those of summits:

High Pike 658
Hare Stones 627
Miton Hill 607
Round Knott 603
Carrock Fell 661

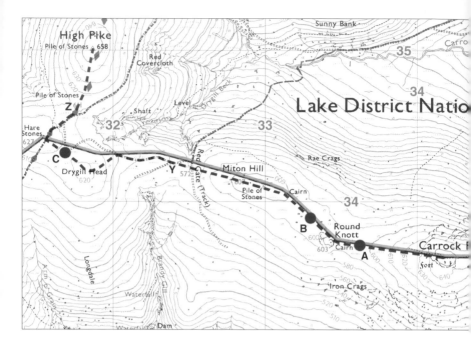

Fig 28: Calculating height gain

There are other known heights, too, namely those that are spot heights:

611, south of High Pike (Point Z)
572, west of Miton Hill (Point Y)

But some intermediate heights – those marked on the map with a red circle – are not known. In this example, they are not hugely significant, but if you imagined a height difference of several hundred metres between each of the known and unknown points on the map, you begin to see why it becomes important to bring these unknown heights into the equation.

So, what can you do? The only answer is to arrive at a best estimate. Let's consider each in turn:

Point A – lies between the 600 metre contour on Carrock Fell and the 600 metre contour on Round Knott. The contour lines to the north and south of this point are 590 metres. So, Point A lies between 590 metres and 600 metres. The only reasonable option is to call Point A 595metres.

Point B – is exactly the same, for the same reasons, 595 metres.

Point C – lies between the 620 metres contour on Drygill Head, and the 620 metres contour on Hare Stones. The next lowest contour line is 610 metres. So, Point C becomes 615 metres.

Now the only other unknown height is that of Drygill Head. In reality you would not visit Drygill Head, but use that track just to the north of it; it is included here for demonstration purposes. Drygill Head is higher than 620 metres. There are no more contour rings. The next contour up would have been 630 metres. So, you make an assumption: Drygill Head is 625 metres.

To complete the calculation you must do some adding and subtracting.

To begin you can ignore the height of High Pike, as we are descending from it. In fact, you can ignore all the descents, unless you want to know that information too.

The calculation for **height gain** starts at Point Z – 611 metres. Now:

Ascend to Hare Stones (627) = 16 metres
Point C (615) to Drygill Head (625) = 10 metres
Point Y (572) to Miton Hill (607) = 35 metres
Point B (595) to Round Knott (603) = 8 metres
Point A (595) to Carrock Fell (661) = 66 metres

The total height gain then is 135 metres. Had you simply taken the height difference between Point Z and the top of Carrock Fell the answer would have been just 50 metres which is quite different.

Going in the opposite direction, from Carrock Fell to High Pike, the height gain is 132 metres. See if you can work it out for yourself.

Does this system work everywhere?

Unfortunately, there are places where calculating height gain in this manner is just impossible. Look at the map on the next page (Figure 29). It shows a section of the Cuillin Ridge on the Isle of Skye, a stretch of mountainous countryside so complex there simply is not room for the information needed to help calculate height gain.

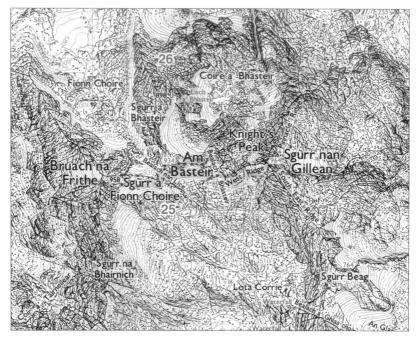

Fig 29: Cuillin Ridge, Isle of Skye

The last word

In the above illustrations, the start and finish heights were different places. So, height gain and the amount of descent (height loss) would be different. But if you start and finish at exactly the same spot, the height gain and height loss are equal, regardless of which way you travel.

Reading and interpreting maps

Perhaps the most important skill to be learned at an early stage is to understand what the map is telling you; what kind of terrain you are looking at. First impressions often tell you a lot, but then you need to study the map in greater detail. It may look confusing, but a map is a treasure trove of information, and understanding what the information on the map is saying will better equip you to deal with situations on the ground.

Fig 30: Extract from Outdoor Leisure Map 5, showing Kidsty Pike and Riggindale, Lake District

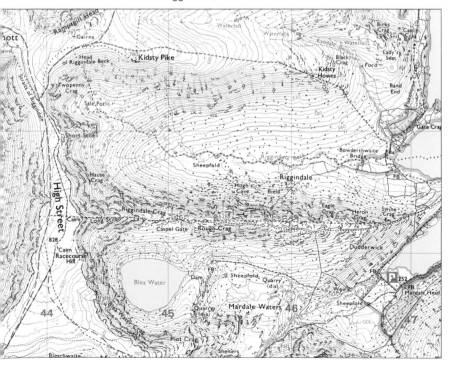

A sense of relief

We can look at two examples. Figure 30 (previous page) shows a rugged part of the Lake District; Figure 33 on page 55, shows an extract from the Chilterns, quite a different landscape picture.

What does the Lake District extract say about the landscape?

First impressions:
- closely packed contour lines that indicate steep slopes

- some less steep ground, shown by the more spaced-out contour lines. This is upland, so the contour interval is 10 metres

- streams and lakes

- quite a lot of craggy and bouldery terrain

- a few rights of way, but that is not so much a problem because the strong brown line along the edge of the lake (actually Haweswater Reservoir) shows that this is mainly Access Land.

A closer look shows:
- the land is falling west to east; you can tell that by the contour heights leading up to Kidsty Pike

- the highest ground is in the west, around High Street

- there are few clearly defined summits; most are simply rounded uplifts above the adjacent land

- north of High Street a gentle slope is flanked by very steep ground. This is a descending **ridge**, and leads north to a very narrow neck of land, a **saddle**, called the Straits of Riggindale

- from the saddle, the land to the north-west descends irregularly around The Knott, although the western slope of High Street, as it falls to Hayeswater, is quite uniform

- from the saddle, the land to the north-east actually climbs around the rim of the valley to the east, Riggindale

- a very narrow ridge runs from Mardale Head almost exactly east–west to the top of High Street. This is Rough Crag; the name should also tell you something. The ridge is very narrow, with tightly packed contour lines pressing in from the north and south; it is also rocky on both flanks

- although the Rough Crag ridge has a right of way shown along it, if you look closely you can see the dashed line of a path, which initially sets off from the east by keeping to the south of a boundary (a wall, in fact). Since the marked right of way seems to tangle with some rocky ground to the north of the wall, you might reasonably expect to find yourself on the dotted path rather than the right of way. In fact, the right of way is virtually unwalkable; attempting it is not recommended. But it is worth making the point here that religiously sticking to the course of a 'green' right of way is not always the best plan. Look closely at the map; do not make assumptions, or you may have assumed that the path along Rough Crag was to the north of the wall, when, in fact, it's to the south. That can make quite a difference in poor visibility

- the ridge of Rough Crag becomes very steep as it adjoins High Street, to the west of the tiny pond at Caspel Gate

- the **height difference** between the starting point at Mardale Head and High Street summit is 576 metres. Of course that is not the same as **height gain**; there is a slight descent from the top of Rough Crag to Caspel Gate, and likewise from Kidsty Pike to the Straits of Riggindale, and this will affect your calculations.

If High Street was your objective, you might prefer to consider the rather easier option over Kidsty Pike. Certainly the gradient looks a lot more manageable, but it is clearly farther to walk. This is where you start weighing up all of the above information to decide on the route you would take.

'Planning a walk' is discussed in the next chapter; suffice to say here that the best circuit to make would be up Rough Crag first to High Street, then north and round to Kidsty Pike, then descending from there. Unfortunately, this sort of information is not found on maps because it introduces other dimensions – pleasure, effort and reward – a rugged and energetic start to a major summit, followed by a more relaxed descent. Perfect.

Fig 31: Riggindale

These two pictures show some of the terrain in question. Figure 31 is looking down into Riggindale – that deeply incised valley between the **ridge** of Rough Crag on the right, and the slopes rising to Kidsty Pike on the left.

Fig 32: Descending to the Straits of Riggindale

Simply by studying the map, try to develop a mental image of what the landscape looks like. At first it isn't easy, but gradually it does all begin to make sense. The same is true of that of Figure 32, which shows the ground falling from High Street (behind the photographer) towards the **saddle** of the Straits of Riggindale.

It takes a good deal of practice to relate what you see on the map to what you eventually see on the ground. Part of the initial problem is that the compression of the map over-exaggerates the narrowness of some features. Rough Crag, for example, looks frighteningly narrow in places, yet you can see from the picture that there's really plenty of room to walk. This is not always the case; ridges can become desperately narrow at times.

Now let's consider the second map (Figure 33), which shows a walk in the Chilterns.

First impressions:
- much gentler countryside, with contours widely spaced; but remember, because this is comparatively low-lying land, the contour interval is 5 metres not 10 metres

- considerably more woodland

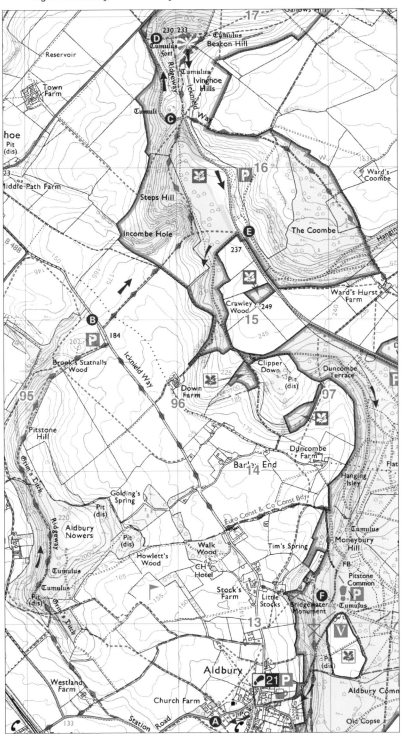

Fig 33: Extract from the Pathfinder® Guide Chilterns and Thames Valley

- field boundaries

- roads

- some steep ground, especially to the north.

A closer look shows:
- the woodland is a mix of pine and broadleaf

- the highest point seems to be at the edge of Crawley Wood, but that generally the land falls to the south, towards Aldbury

- in the north, the land gathers sufficiently steeply to create a small peak, Ivinghoe Beacon (a fabulous viewpoint, which is what the circular blue symbol tells you).

Follow the route round, starting in Aldbury and going in a clockwise direction, and see if you can interpret what the map is telling you about the landscape at each stage. You should not expect to spot everything just yet; you are just trying to get a feel for the lie of the land.

What is not immediately obvious from this map extract – you need the whole map to understand fully – is that where the contours gather together to form a stretch of steep ground, it actually makes what is known as an **escarpment**, a place where higher land, generally flatter,

Fig 34: The Cleveland Hills escarpment

suddenly drops (or rises, depending on your point of view), and in effect creates an edge. Escarpments are common features of the British landscape and occur not only in the Chilterns, but in the Brecon Beacons of South Wales, in the Peak District, in North Yorkshire, even in Lancashire. Escarpments are excellent walking country, providing a lofty vantage point with good views over the surrounding countryside. Take a look at Figure 34, which shows a walker below the spectacular escarpment of the Cleveland Hills in North Yorkshire.

On the spur of the moment

Quite often the contours appear to go off in all directions, twisting this way and that, and it is not always easy to figure out where the valleys are. Of course, if there's a stream or a river shown, then that is a good clue, but in limestone country especially you might find large expanses with little evidence of watercourses.

> *If the Vs or Us point uphill, it is a valley. If the Vs or Us point downhill, you're looking at a spur.*

Once again the clue to the solution lies in the contour heights shown on the map, remembering that the top of the number points uphill. If you now look at Figure 35, you can see that the contours of the valleys and the adjacent spurs have a rough V or U shape.

Fig 35: Spurs and valleys

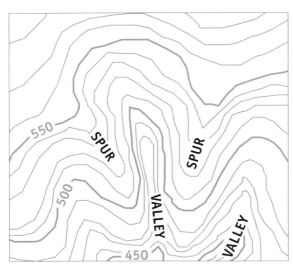

Planning
a walk

It may be argued that it makes more sense at this point to take maps outside and begin the process of relating them to the landscape. But working out walks on a map is a continuing part of the process begun in the preceding chapter, that of learning to read what the map is telling you. And the ability to plan attractive walks is part of that development. For many it is as enjoyable as the walk itself. In fact, each year hardy backpackers set off alone or in small groups to walk from one side of Scotland to the other following no set route. They spend months planning their own route, tweaking it here and there, working out bad weather alternatives, reading the nuances of the map, deciding where to camp or spend the night. The anticipatory pleasure in doing just that is considerable, and all the more so when you actually get out there, faithfully follow the route you planned, or making changes if the weather dictates that you should, and everything turns out fine.

 Planning is the key to a successful walk.

A walk is not just the process of putting one foot in front of the other; it is everything from the detailed planning, weighing up the options, calculating distance and time, getting out there and doing it, and then coming home to a hot bath and a drop of whatever makes you feel good.

A walk is a package.

What sort of walk are you planning?

There are many considerations to take into account when planning a walk, but they fall into two broad headings:

Subjective: those where you make the decisions and the choices, and
Objective: those over which you have no control.

Subjective aspects involve making decisions about:
- where you are intending to walk

- whether the walk is circular, out-and-back or linear – in the last case you will need to consider the transport logistics

- what distance you want to cover

- how much 'climbing' you want to include

- the extent to which you can keep the walk on footpaths rather than roads

- whether some footpaths more than others offer better views, take you through attractive villages, to popular beauty spots, or past pubs (or avoids these, if that is your preference)

- what 'escape routes' – see below – there are.

Objective considerations are:
- the weather – though you do have the choice of looking at the weather forecast and deciding to abort the walk if things look grim

- the terrain you will encounter – although you can go some way to assessing the type of terrain you will be crossing, when you finally get to grips with it you are invariably faced with aspects that just do not show on the map, e.g. knee-deep heather, land that is flooded after heavy rainfall, seasonal overgrowth, obstructions

- accidents – while everyone hopes that accidents will not happen, sadly they sometimes do, and the person planning the walk needs to know the quickest and safest route to safety from virtually any stage of the walk

- changes in the weather – the day may start fine, but the British climate is unpredictable at best. The same 'escape route' planning that applies to potential accidents applies to the need to deal with sudden and unexpected adverse weather also.

There is another consideration, too. It is vitally important to devise a route that is not only within the physical ability of everyone involved, but also *within the map reader's competence*. Following field edges and country lanes in rural Oxfordshire is one thing, navigating across trackless moorland in the Western Highlands with the mist closing in is quite another.

The process of learning to map read and navigate is an incremental thing that adopts the walk-before-you-run philosophy. Take it, literally, one step at a time, and remember the word KISS – Keep It Stupidly Simple, or, if you prefer, Keep It Simple, Stupid!

The planning process

Having decided on your aims for the walk, it is time to start planning with a map. Once you have decided where you are going and have the relevant map, there are basically four stages:

1. Identify the 'attractive' stretches you would like to include
Having understood what the information on the map is telling you, you start to get a feel for what the area you are intending to visit is like. Use a highlighter pen to pinpoint the appealing stretches, and if you particularly want to include a pub along the way then you will already have noticed that the Ordnance Survey *Explorer* maps do have a pub symbol. What the map does not tell you is what the beer or the food is like – there is just so much a map can do, after all.

2. Make connections
Look for the footpaths that connect the places you want to visit, noting any alternatives that may be possible, and gradually tease out a connection so that your route starts to take shape. Be prepared to revise your plans; the more you study the map, the more you see. You are trying to develop a walk that satisfies the aims you identified above, and with experience you acquire a feel for walks that meet your needs.

3. Is it good for you?
You next need to consciously assess the route against your aims.
- Is it the right length?

- Is the format what you wanted, e.g. circular or linear?
- Does it seem to be within the ability of those taking part?
- If it is a linear walk, what can you do about transport, e.g. is the finishing point on a bus route and will the buses be running?

4. Make adjustments

If the route is too long, find a way of reducing it – maybe start at a different point, or take a short cut. If part of it looks too steep, find a way round that section. Keep repeating the process until you get the route you want.

TIP: There is one other little bit of planning you can do at this stage that has nothing to do with maps or route planning. Research. Do a little background research about the places you are visiting on the walk. This is a travel journalist's trick. There is nothing worse than spending a couple of hours exploring a castle, coming away and then discovering something even more fascinating tucked away in a nearby woodland.

How long will it take?

Does it matter? Well, yes, it does. And, no, it doesn't.

Imagine this: it's a lovely day, perfect for walking and everything is going exactly according to plan. Your map reading is spot on. You take a break by a stream and dangle your feet. Stop for coffee and a bite. There's a car and a change of clothing at the end of the walk. The sky is blue; the birds are singing.

Why do you want it to end? Does it matter how long the walk takes?

On the other hand: same scenario, except there isn't a car waiting. You have to catch a bus back to the start. It's the last bus. You can't afford to miss it.

Does it matter how long the walk takes? It does now; the consequences of missing that last bus may not be life threatening, but are you up to walking all the way back to the start in growing darkness?

Walking speed

The more walking you do, the better you become at roughly calculating how long the walk will take; you get to know your own abilities. So, on familiar terrain, 'distance' may be all you need to know to give you a fairly accurate idea of how much time to allow. Moreover, you get to know the length of walk that best suits you, whether it is 16 kilometres (10 miles) for a day-long walk, or 6 kilometres ($3\frac{3}{4}$ miles) for an afternoon stroll.

Walking speed is a personal thing, geared not only to what you can physically achieve and can sustain for prolonged periods, but also to what you want to do. Walking is a recreation, not military training. Much as we might admire those super-fit army types who can romp across 80 kilometres (50 miles) and still have the energy for an hour in the gym, that is not what recreational walking is about. So, at one extreme you may find that, if you needed to, you could push on at 6 or 7km/hour ($3\frac{3}{4}$–4 mph); at the other extreme you might be perfectly happy at 3km/hour (2 mph).

But that is far from true of everyone. Each of us has a comfortable walking speed; go beyond that and things start to become uncomfortable, leading to tiredness and lowering of morale.

Of course, 'walking speed' assumes continuous progress, but makes no allowance for:
- voluntary stops, e.g. snack breaks, bird-watching, eating blackberries, calls of nature, 'other' distractions
- particularly difficult terrain
- pathless walking sections
- poor conditions underfoot, e.g. mud, ice, snow
- strong winds
- heavy loads
- unreliable knees.

Naismith's Rule

This simple rule has been in use for years; it is a good guide, but it is a worthwhile exercise to keep notes over a period of a few months and assess the time your walks actually take against Naismith's calculation. You may find that you are 10 per cent faster than Naismith, or 15 per cent slower. The value of this is that you can then always apply Naismith's Rule to your walks, and make this adjustment for your personal abilities.

The rule simply states that you allow one hour for each 5 kilometre (3 miles) of distance. Then add half an hour for each 300 metre

(1,000 feet) of ascent (if you are planning your walk using a map with contours at 10 metre intervals, that conveniently breaks down to one minute for each contour line crossed).

Naismith's Rule applies only to those parts of the route that ascend; with descents it is assumed that they do not significantly affect your speed. But lengthy, steep descents, especially across poor ground, can really slow you down, and you need to add more time for this: around half of the time calculated for the ascents.

Of course, if your walk involves no significant ascents, then Naismith's Rule is needlessly rigorous. It is vital to know how long you think a walk should take, but a better idea evolves over a period of time of your own abilities: 16 kilometres (10 miles) on the flat = 'x' hours; 16 kilometres (10 miles) with a lot of ascent = 'y' hours.

Any problems?

The main problem with planning from a map is that you cannot be sure the footpaths are open, unobstructed and straightforward to follow. In some remote areas paths may have fallen into disuse. In farming areas, fields may be ploughed over or full of cattle (including bulls); both may be a deterrent to progress.

When planning a walk in an area that is new to you, mark up alternative routes in case you find your preferred route is in some way blocked.

Guidebook walks

One of the surest ways of developing your walk-planning skills is to use a *Pathfinder® Guide* or *Crimson Short Walks*. These are regularly updated and use the very latest mapping, in full colour. They are compiled and revised by a team of professional outdoor writers (many of them members of the Outdoor Writers and Photographers Guild – see www.owpg.org.uk). A guidebook walk lets you see how the writer planned the route. You can decide for yourself whether you agree with his or her decisions, but using a guidebook will take all the effort out of planning, except to the extent that you may use the guidebook walk as a basis from which to extend the route to suit your own wishes.

Ultimately, a guidebook is just that, a guide, and is intended to encourage independent and more widespread exploration. It takes the uncertainty out of walk planning, and, as a rule, is only affected by changes that have occurred subsequent to publication.

Think ahead

When setting off on a walk it is a potentially life-saving practice to leave a note of your intended route and *the time you think the walk will take* with someone who can alert the emergency services if you fail to return reasonably close to your intended return time. Of course, this is not always possible, there may be no one you can leave a note with, and in any case this can fall foul of a number of seemingly irrelevant issues, like a decision to stop off at a pub, or to add some extra mileage, or the simple fact that it was a lovely day and you did not want the walk to end.

Using maps

H aving understood what a map is, and what all the marginal data means, it is now appropriate to begin the basic skills of navigation: how to use the map.

Setting the map

For the greater part of your walking you will constantly be relating the map in your hand to the ground you are walking, and vice versa. This is fundamental to navigation, it is ongoing, there is no end to it, it's something you do all the time. In fact, you would be silly not to.

'Setting the map' simply means holding the map so that the features on it roughly (ideally exactly) correspond with what you see in front of you, to the sides and even behind you.

Why is it important? Well, for a start, you need to take the correct route out of the car park.

There are two ways you can set the map. The first uses a compass (a gadget that will be more fully discussed in the next chapter); the other sets the map by the features around you.

Setting the map using a compass

To set the map using a compass, there are three steps (see Figure 36):

1. Set the N on the compass dial so that it aligns with the big arrow at the top of the compass.

2. Hold the compass on your map – near the edge is easier – so that the long edge of the compass is aligned with the grid lines on the map, and pointing north (not east!), i.e. to the top of the map.

3. Keep a tight hold of both map and compass, and, holding them horizontally, turn the whole map (and yourself) until the red end of the compass needle is aligned with the red arrow inside the circular dial.

Fig 36: The three steps in setting the map

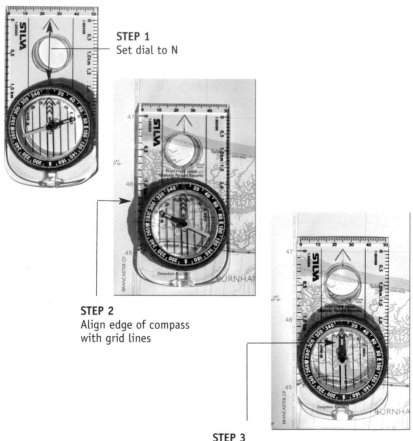

STEP 1
Set dial to N

STEP 2
Align edge of compass
with grid lines

STEP 3
Spin map and compass together to align
needle with 'North' arrow in the dial

The map is now set, the top edge of the map is north, the left edge is west, the right, east, and the bottom, south, i.e. behind you. Now you can begin relating what you see in front of you, and all around you, with what you see on the map.

Try it with a few easy landmarks first, like a church steeple or the edge of a woodland or plantation. Of course, the moment you alter your position – if, for example, you spin through 90° – then the map needs to be reset. In fact, you could be resetting the map every time you change direction during a walk. But the more accomplished you become, the less is the need to do this. In any case, if you spend all your time looking at the map, you won't see anything.

Setting a map by features

Using a compass to set a map is by far the most accurate way, but as you become more at ease with using map and compass, so you can quickly learn to set the map simply by relating it to features that you see around you. Setting the map in this way means that you turn the map so that a feature you can see on the ground corresponds with the surrounding landscape in exactly the same relationship as on the map. Of course, it follows that setting a map by reference to features will only work when you can actually see identifiable features.

It is also true that to set a map by features, you need to know where you are in order to start identifying what is around you. But it works the other way, too – unless you are hopelessly lost. You can use that woodland over on the left, and that church with a tower directly ahead and the lake over on the right to give a rough idea of where you are. It isn't precise, but if the map is set, even at this degree of inaccuracy, you can at least stop yourself wandering off in the wrong direction – if you know your route lies between the church and the lake, and you find yourself heading for the woodland, something is wrong.

Finding your way

As you walk, map in hand, you are constantly checking your position. You will find that you do keep track of your progress, but every so often you need to confirm exactly where you are, especially if a choice of routes lies ahead.

It is very reassuring (and confidence-building) to realise just how frequently you get the map reading right. As a 'novice' navigator, you should check the map every time you make a major change of direction, but then less frequently, as you become more experienced.

In time you are almost subconsciously ticking off what might be called 'reassurance points': field boundary junctions, farms, rivers and streams – even the most able navigators do this, regularly. It will (should) be something you do every time you go for a walk. But what if some of the features you are looking for are missing? There will be one of three possible reasons:

- You are not at the position you pinpointed, i.e. temporarily lost.

- You made a mistake in plotting the position during the planning stage.

- You are at the pinpoint position, but what you're looking for has been removed. Usually this is a field boundary, but it can also be something much larger, like a building that tumbled down and was finally removed. It takes a long time for changes like this to find their way onto new mapping.

If you are in the correct position, then there will often be enough other features nearby – walls, and especially the shape of walls – to help you to position yourself. Often the best navigational aids are there in front of you – walls and fences, and, more to the point, the way they bend or suddenly change direction, and, of course, the path itself, waymarks and signposts. You can find totally barren and signpostless Britain if you try hard enough. But mostly, it isn't.

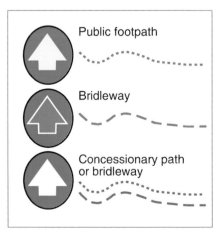

Public footpath

Bridleway

Concessionary path or bridleway

Routes across farmland are often waymarked, and the type of waymark links in with the three principal routes as depicted on maps. Figure 37 shows the map delineation from Ordnance Survey *Explorer* maps.

Fig 37: Conventional waymarks and corresponding map depiction for footpaths and bridleways

Signposts also abound, and are usually found at major

Fig 38: Without this signpost on Sleights Moor in the North York Moors, Coast-to-Coast walkers may well miss the turning

changes of route direction, and track or path junctions (see Figure 38). Stand beside a signpost at a known path junction, and, as with a trig pillar, you know exactly where you are.

When walking with a map, always rotate the map so that the route you are following is going away from you. This way, you will not mix up 'lefts' and 'rights'.

Introducing the compass

There is nothing mystical about a compass. At its basic level, a compass consists of a magnetised pointer free to align itself accurately with the Earth's magnetic field. The Chinese are credited with 'inventing' the compass in AD271, one of the four great inventions of ancient China, although there are references in Chinese literature to magnetism 2,500 years ago.

Modern hand-held compasses use a magnetised needle or dial inside a fluid-filled capsule; the fluid causes the needle to 'dampen' rather than oscillate back and forth around magnetic north.

Most modern recreational compasses integrate a protractor with the compass, using a separate magnetised needle. In this design the rotating housing containing the magnetised needle is fitted with orienting lines and an orienting arrow, then mounted in a transparent baseplate containing a direction-of-travel (DOT) indicator for use in taking bearings directly from a map.

Other features include map and romer scales for measuring distances and plotting positions on maps, luminous markings or bezels for use at night or in poor light, various sighting mechanisms for taking bearings of distant objects with greater precision, 'global' needles for use in differing hemispheres, adjustable declination for obtaining instant true bearings without resorting to arithmetic, and devices such as inclinometers for measuring gradients.

But surely all you need to know is which way is 'North'? This is true, but if a compass can help in other ways, then that is better value for money.

The first rules of navigation

There are four basic rules:
Rule 1: Buy a compass.
Rule 2: Learn how to use it.
Rule 3: Always have it with you when out walking.
Rule 4: Trust it.

There is nothing difficult about reading and using a compass, so do not persuade yourself otherwise. Let's start by looking at the basics of the compass – see Figure 39.

Scale: In this illustration, the scale is in centimetres, but it could equally be in millimetres. This sort of scale ruler is useful in

Fig 39: Basic compass

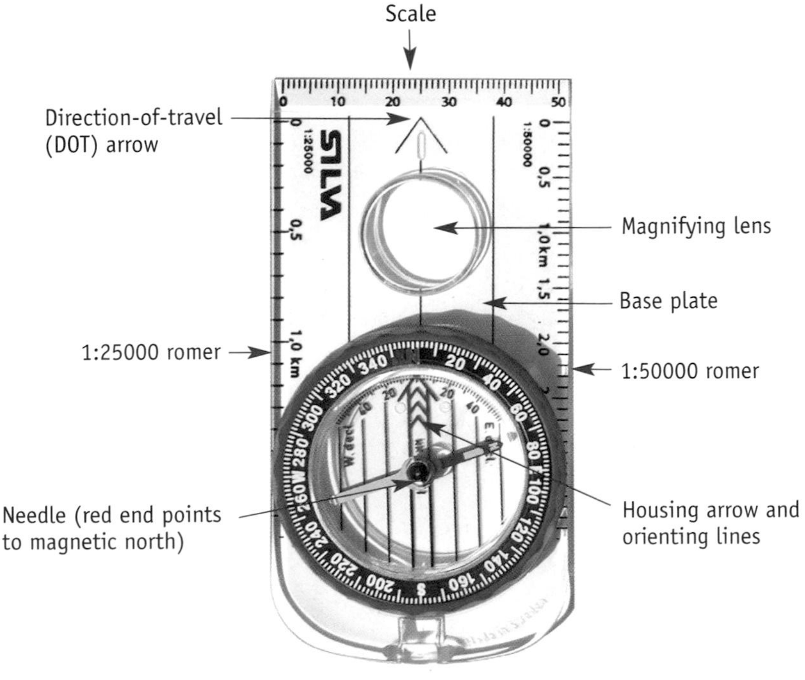

calculating distance against a map. To do that, you need to know that with 1:25000 maps, 4 centimetres equals 1 kilometre; on 1:50000 maps, 2 centimetres equals 1 kilometre. NOTE: The particular compass used in this illustration also has romers down each side, one at a scale of 1:25000 and the other at 1:50000 which, in this respect, make the scale along the top less vital. But not all compasses have romers. If your compass does not have romers, you might consider buying one that does; it saves you having to remember whether it is 2 or 4 centimetres that equal 1 kilometre.

Magnifying glass: You may take the view that there is nothing wrong with your eyesight, but for most of us that will not always be the case. That little circular lens helps with the fine detail of maps, especially to show routes, for example, through farmyards or which side of a field boundary a path follows. A magnifying lens is not essential, but if you are buying a new compass, then buy one with a lens.

Base plate: Nothing magical here; that's all it is, a base plate.

Housing arrow and orienting lines: This is the compass housing. Inside it sits the **compass needle**. The housing, which rotates easily, is filled with a liquid which 'dampens' the needle's movement, otherwise the needle swings to and fro for ages.

Sometimes, mainly because of changes in atmospheric pressure caused by being at higher altitude, a bubble will develop in the liquid. If the bubble is small and has no effect on the swing of the needle, you can continue to use the compass. But if the bubble is large, you need a new compass. It's like a waterproof watch: once you get water in there, you cannot get it out – it's the same with compass bubbles, which remain stubbornly in the housing even when you go back to lower altitudes.

Underneath the needle are the orienting lines, the lines that allow you to line up the compass housing with grid lines on a map. The two central lines are drawn as an arrow. This is the housing arrow, and it points to wherever you turn the housing to point to, although it is a good idea always to return it to north. Around the edge of the housing are the cardinal points of the compass – North, South, East and West – and smaller sub-divisions of 2°, marked up at 20° intervals.

Needle: Typically red (and sometimes also luminous) at the north end and black or white at the other.

Direction-of-travel (DOT) arrow: The DOT arrow runs through the magnifying lens from the edge of the compass housing. This is the bit of the compass that will point you in the direction you need to take.

Types of compass

There are various types of compass, and you get what you pay for. If you want to, you can buy a sighting compass like that shown in Figure 40.

But before you invest in one of the more sophisticated compasses that are available on the market, it makes sense to start with something uncluttered and uncomplicated like a basic expedition compass – see Figure 41.

Or just a simple field compass – see Figure 42 – is perfectly adequate.

Fig 40: A 'sighting' compass

A small point

If you look closely at Figure 39 on page 71, you'll see that within the housing arrow the letters 'MN'(for Magnetic North) appear. If you never intend to take your compass beyond the northern hemisphere, then you can forget these letters, because they simply tell you that the compass is for use in the northern hemisphere. The southern hemisphere – South Africa, Australia and New Zealand in particular – have 'MS' (Magnetic South) on their compasses, while

Fig 41: An 'expedition' compass

all the rest in the middle have 'ME'. The reason is a little complex, and adds nothing to your understanding of how compasses work in Britain – it is to do with magnetic inclination. If you suspend a bar magnet from a piece of string and allow it to come to rest it will certainly point to magnetic north, but it will not necessarily be perfectly horizontal. The angle at which it comes to rest is called the

Fig 42: A field compass

magnetic inclination, and this varies depending on where you are in the world and its relationship to magnetic north, which as we saw in 'Understanding North', is somewhere off the coast of Canada. A compass from the wrong hemisphere will not function properly elsewhere because of this magnetic inclination.

If you are going to a destination outside the northern hemisphere and need a compass, buy a new one when you reach your destination.

How attractive are you?

Because a compass relies on magnetism, many things, including your own personal magnetism, can affect the way the compass works. The usual culprits are cameras around your neck, mobile phone in your breast pocket, metal zips, and even the underwiring in a ladies' bra.

Before you set off on a walk, test the compass by holding it in various positions to see whether anything is affecting the way the needle swings. If the needle is affected, you may need to make adjustments – move the phone to another pocket, for example – or simply hold the compass away from your body.

Magnetic rocks

Having now digested everything you need to know about compasses, there is one more snippet of information that will make all that learning quite useless: magnetic rocks.

In some areas of Britain, notably among the Cuillin on the Isle of Skye, but in other places, too, there are rock types that are high in iron content, and these will affect your compass reading, especially if the magnetic field is particularly strong locally.

Opinions differ about the extent to which this sort of influence affects compass readings. But, when the iron-bearing rocks were lain down as molten lava, millions of years ago, magnetic north was in quite a different location than where you find it now, and it is that old magnetic north that is locked into the rocks, and will deflect compass readings.

Using compasses

Wonderful as compasses are, experienced navigators always make the point that they are no substitute for good map reading skills, merely an additional prop. Good navigators are always checking the route for mapped features as they walk, using these to fix their position as an on-going process. The skill in practical map reading is not to walk for a while and then ask 'Where are we?', but to be constantly checking.

What the compass does is to show remarkably accurate direction on the ground, i.e. the direction of your route, or a distant feature. While there is an abundance of mapped features around you, following a route using just the map is comparatively easy. Where a compass comes into its own is when mapped features are few and far between, or, at the other extreme, there are so many features that they become confusing, making it difficult to decide on the route clearly.

Although a compass is fundamentally a simple device, using it in the early stages of learning navigational skills can be a little daunting and baffling. So, we need to KISS (Keep It Stupidly Simple, remember?). Thankfully, it does not take long to get the hang of it, but regular practice will soon reap its rewards.

The main use for a compass is to tell you which way to go, whenever there is doubt, or as a reassurance factor – just checking. But a compass alone cannot do this. What is needed is to take a **bearing**.

What is a bearing?

A bearing is simply the angle between 'North', where you are and where you want to go. Bearings are defined by expressing the number of degrees (expressed as x°) between 0 and 360 in a clockwise direction from North to the direction of travel. Look at Figure 43.

A bearing is the angle 'x': the angle between 'N', 'A' and 'C' – in this case 40°. So, point C lies on a bearing of 40° from your present position. 'C' might be a distant feature, or simply the continuation of a path you are following which is momentarily out of sight over the brow of a domed field. Equally it may be nothing more complicated than confirming which of a number of paths that converge at your location is the correct one to take.

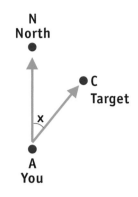

Fig 43: A bearing

Taking a bearing on the map

What you now need to do is to figure out the bearing (A–C) on the map from your known position to your target destination.

There are three steps in taking a bearing :

When calculating a bearing, do a rough estimate first. It does not need to be accurate, between 0 and 90 will suffice. Once you have taken the bearing, if it roughly compares with your 'guesstimate', that is fine; if not, something is wrong.

Step 1: Place your compass on the map so that one of the long edges joins both the point where you are and your destination point (or direction, if it is simply a path), making sure that the DOT arrow is pointing towards (or along) your target.

Step 2: Rotate the compass housing so that the housing arrow is parallel with the N–S grid lines on the map – see Figure 44.

Make sure that in both these steps you are as accurate as possible; cutting down on error now will reduce the risk of difficulty later.

Step 3: Read off the bearing on the compass housing next to the direction-of-travel arrow – see Figure 44.

Fig 44: Use your compass as a protractor to measure the bearing

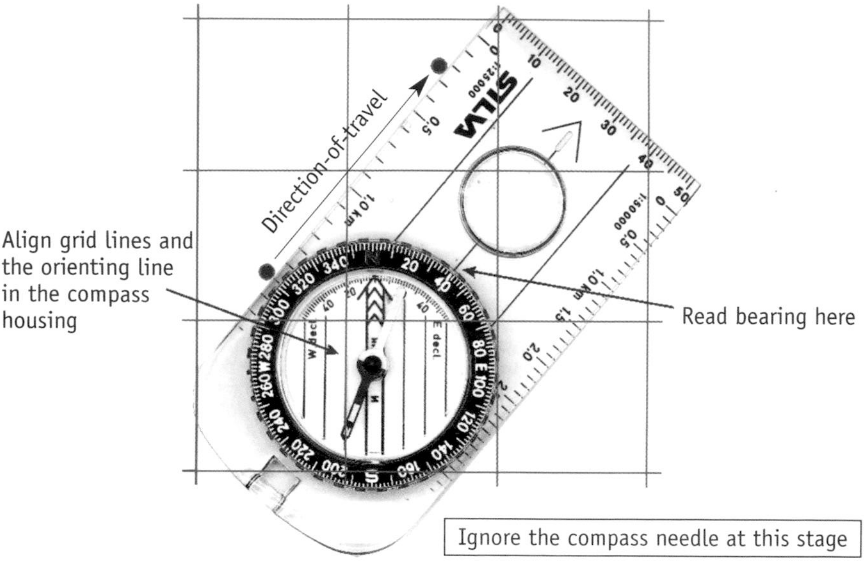

Align grid lines and the orienting line in the compass housing

Direction-of-travel

Read bearing here

Ignore the compass needle at this stage

Some simple mistakes

Everyone makes a few simple mistakes when learning how to use a compass. The main thing is to do the learning in a safe location, not standing in the middle of moorland.

Mistake 1: The compass is not aligned in the direction-of-travel – A to C in Figure 43. If your compass is aligned C to A, you will get a reading that is incorrect by 180°.

Mistake 2: The orienting lines in the compass housing are not aligned to the north of the map. An error of 180° will result again, if you do this the wrong way round.

The importance of accuracy

When working with map and compass it is important to be as accurate as possible – make sure locations are very precisely lined up. Fail to do this and errors will creep in.

But how much of a problem is it? If you are simply trying to determine whether the path in front of you heads off in the right direction, then not much of a problem at all.

If you are deciding between two paths that are fairly close together, it could be more critical, but probably not life threatening.

But if a wall junction to where your route continues is a kilometre distant over the brow of a hill, you need to be sure of your direction.

Or if you are trying to decide between two narrow, descending ridges in poor visibility, then failing to be accurate could result in very serious consequences.

Magnetic variation revisited

'Understanding North' touched briefly on magnetic variation. It is now time to take a closer look.

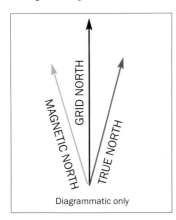

Fig 45: Magnetic variation

Diagrammatic only

Magnetic variation is the difference between **grid north** and **magnetic north** (see Figure 45).

Grid north is at the top of your map; magnetic north is wandering about the frozen wastes of northern Canada, slowly moving east. Moreover, the direction of magnetic north varies depending on where you are. *But* for the foreseeable future, magnetic grid is west of grid north. How far west is indicated in the marginal data on maps. Ordnance Survey *Explorer* Map 296 states: *Magnetic north is estimated at 3'01" west of grid north for July 2006. Annual change is approximately 11" east.* As Ordnance Survey maps are produced at different intervals, and relate to different parts of the country, you will find that information about magnetic variation is different on each map. If you want to know the magnetic variation for any part of the country then you can visit www.nearby.org.uk which links through to the website for the British

Geological Society where there is a magnetic variation calculator.

For the purposes of this book, magnetic variation can be taken as a little under 4° west.

Is that far? And does it matter? You can do the mathematics if you wish, but the fact is that over a distance of a kilometre, a 4° error will put you 70 metres off course. Close enough, in good visibility and a safe location, but how would you feel about being 70 metres adrift in thick mist on a windswept moor or a mountain ridge? Add to this the fact that most compasses are made to be accurate to a tolerance of ± 4°, and you could be 140 metres out. How critical is that?

Walking with a compass

Now that you understand how to take bearings, it is time to go out so that you can start putting what you've learned into practice.

First, we have calculated what magnetic variation is, but what do we do with it?

Need we bother with magnetic variation at all?

We saw in the last chapter that a 4° variation will have a 70 metres deviation over a distance of 1 kilometre. It therefore follows that as the distance, i.e. the 1 kilometre, gets less, so the 'error' is less. And if all you are doing is checking which of two paths a few strides in front of you is the correct one to follow, you can safely ignore magnetic variation altogether. You can also ignore it when setting the map (see 'Using maps'). But conversely the greater the distance you need to travel on a bearing, the greater the risk of error, and the greater the need to allow for magnetic variation.

One solution would be to ensure that each 'leg' on which you are using a bearing is shorter rather than longer. Of course this may not always be possible because at the end of each leg you need to be somewhere that you can accurately identify on the map, e.g. a field boundary corner. But if there is nothing at all, you have no choice but to navigate over a longer distance. In this circumstance, magnetic variation does play a role, and the need to be very accurate comes into play.

How to allow for magnetic variation

When you take a bearing using your compass and the map, i.e. you have taken a bearing from your known position to a distant point, then the bearing you have taken is called a **grid bearing**, because it is taken from the grid on the map. Now you need to allow for magnetic variation.

The same is true if you are not entirely sure of your position, and want to use your compass to take a bearing of a distant feature, e.g. a building, and then want to use it to trace your position. This bearing, because you took it without reference to the map, i.e. just using magnetism, is called a **magnetic bearing**, a topic that will be returned to shortly.

Many people, and not just those who are learning the skills of map and compass work, find it confusing to remember what to do about magnetic variation. Clearly, if you think about it, if you take a bearing on a map, it will not be the same bearing as the one you take – assuming you can see your target – just using the compass. So, there is a little saying to remember whether to add or subtract that 4° (or whatever) of magnetic variation, and it works:

Men Generally Say Great Minds Agree	M-G-S G-M-A	Magnetic to Grid Subtract Grid to Magnetic Add

So, if you have taken a bearing on a map (grid bearing), say 40°, then to convert to a compass bearing you need to *add* magnetic variation (4°), to give 44°. And that is the compass bearing you now walk along.

There is another way that will be discussed shortly, but for now we need to know how to walk with a compass on a bearing.

Walking on a bearing

You have taken a bearing on a map of, say, 65°. You have added 4° to allow for magnetic variation to give 69° – see Figure 46.

Hold the compass, as level as possible (as shown in Figure 47).

Now, without touching the compass housing, and holding the compass level, spin your entire body round until the compass needle lines up with the north arrow (red on red) – Figure 48.

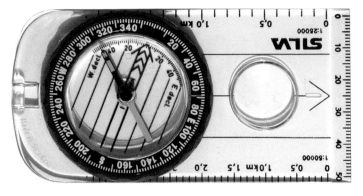

Fig 46: The compass is set on your grid bearing 65°, and magnetic variation (4°) has been added

When you have done this, the direction-of-travel arrow will now point the way to walk. (So, off you go.)

That alternative technique for coping with magnetic variation mentioned earlier is one orienteers use. Instead of worrying about whether to add or subtract magnetic variation, they set the compass to the grid bearing (65° in this example), and simply point the compass needle to 4° west instead of north. The effect is the same.

Fig 47: Hold the compass level, slightly away from your body, to allow for 'personal' magnetism, but not too far. Keep your elbows tucked in

Fig 48: The compass is now aligned to north (red on red)

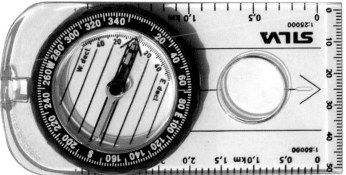

Is it that easy?

If all you wanted the bearing for was to choose between two or more footpaths a short distance in front of you, then, yes, it is that easy.

But if you took the bearing because your target was out of sight over the brow of a hill, then you need some intermediate reference point to be sure you are taking the right line. This reference point needs to be something you can positively identify and which will not move (so not a sheep).

See Figure 49 – the direction-of-travel lies across this heather moor, and the distant mound can be used as an intermediate objective. If the mound is also shown on the map – in this case it is a known tumulus – then that is a bonus because you can recalculate your direction once you get to the mound. But quite often the terrain is not so accommodating, and you must continue to walk along your bearing, looking for new intermediate reference points as you go.

Fig 49: Look for a 'target' along the direction you want to travel

The important thing is that the intermediate reference point is on your bearing, and not off to one side. Experienced navigators can learn to cope with things not being perfectly aligned, but it is a 'no-go zone' for anyone less practised. This process of 'looking ahead' is a vital part of skilful navigation. Not only is it important, as here, with actual navigation, but it is a key part of the state of total awareness that is essential to successful walking.

Once you have identified an intermediate reference point, put your compass away, taking care not to disturb its setting (or make a note of your bearing, just in case), and then walk to your objective. On rough ground it is important to see where you are putting your feet, while on a smooth, grassy hillside you want to enjoy the walk. When you get to the intermediate objective, take out the compass and repeat the whole process until you get to where you are going.

 Trust your compass, not your intuition.

While navigating in this way across fairly easy terrain in good conditions, things are straightforward. But poor visibility and tiredness can disorientate you and persuade you that the compass is somehow giving a wrong reading. If you have done everything correctly, do not be tempted to over-ride your compass; it never gets tired, and always points to north.

Taking a back bearing

To develop confidence in what you are doing, it is useful to use a back bearing to check on your progress. Taking back bearings, however, assumes that you can still see where you started your current leg of the journey from – if you cannot, you are on your own. But, if your start point is still visible, then, without altering anything on the compass, simply spin round so that the white end of the needle points to the red housing arrow (white on red). The direction-of-travel arrow will now point back the way you came.

 Summary

1. Place the edge of the compass on your map so that it joins where you are and where you want to go.

2. Ensure that the direction-of-travel arrow is pointing in the direction you want to go.

3. Turn the compass housing so that the orienting lines are parallel with the vertical grid lines on the map.

4. Read the bearing against the direction-of-travel arrow and add the magnetic variation shown in the map's marginal data.
[NOTE: If magnetic variation is east of grid north rather than west of it, then you would subtract magnetic variation not add it.]

5. Spin yourself bodily around so that the red end of the compass needle lines up with the red housing arrow.

6. The direction-of-travel arrow now points the way to go.

7. Look along your direction-of-travel and identify a feature along the bearing that you can safely walk to.

Can anything go wrong?

There are five steps to ensuring that there is nothing wrong with your technique:

1. Position your compass edge *precisely* between where you are and where you want to go.

2. Ensure the direction-of-travel arrow points in the right direction when you are doing Step 1.

3. Take care to avoid pointing the housing arrow to the bottom of the map – the housing arrow points north, to the top of the map.

4. Make proper allowance for magnetic variation.

5. Ensure the compass orienting lines are *exactly* parallel with the map grid lines.

Some basic techniques

The skills of advanced navigation all derive from the basics contained in this book. But it is important to ensure that these basics are fully understood before venturing into the sort of terrain (and conditions) where more sophisticated techniques are needed. The fundamentals of map reading and basic navigation must become second nature. But there is no mystery to advanced navigation, just the importance of getting the basics right first.

So, this chapter offers a few additional techniques that will be useful. None of what follows is an exact science, and much of it varies from person to person.

Estimating distance on the ground

Experienced golfers can calculate distances to the green on a golf course with incredible accuracy. But for most people, the ability to estimate distance is not easy. Anyone who ever ran 100 metres at school, can make a fair stab at visualising the track distance on any terrain. But with greater distances, being able to look out across a landscape and estimate how far it is to a particular feature is difficult. Nor can it be taught; only practice makes perfect.

Pacing

Imagine that you are on some moorland track from which your intended route diverts after 250 metres. You need to be sure when you have travelled that distance, and 'pacing' is a way of getting it remarkably accurate. But everyone's pace length is different, and everyone's pace is affected by varying terrain. So, you have to begin by seeing how many double paces you personally take for a given distance.

Find a level stretch of ground near home, and see how many double paces, i.e. left foot (or right foot) hitting the ground, you take to cover, say, 100 metres. Test it a few times, to arrive at an average. For most people of average height it will be around 65, but we come in different shapes and sizes, so working out your own stride pattern is important if this technique is to be used. If you have a partner with whom you intend to walk, then get them to check the pacing as well, so that when you are out on the hill both of you can do the pacing. Four legs are better than two.

As an example, if you need to leave a path after 250 metres, you now know that you have to take 65 + 65 + 32½ double paces. That will put you there or thereabouts. But your stride pattern will be affected by slopes, difficult terrain, especially deep heather, and even fatigue, so you will need to make allowance for this.

Dealing with obstacles

Pacing comes into its own on boggy moorland, when your intended route may be barred by a small lake or expanse of boggy ground. If you can see where you are heading this is not so much of a problem, but if you are walking on a bearing you need to know how to negotiate the obstacle, and get back on course.

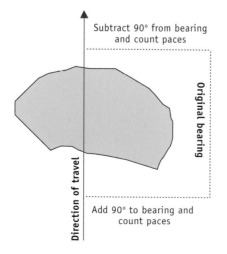

Fig 50: Pacing around an obstacle

Look at Figure 50. You are walking on a bearing and encounter an obstacle, in this case a small lake or pond. It is important that you do not lose your original bearing, and that you get back exactly on course.

To negotiate the obstacle, add exactly 90° to your bearing, and walk along this, *counting your paces as you go,* until you are clear of the end of the obstacle. Now revert to your original bearing, and walk until you are beyond the end of the obstacle. Then subtract 90° from your original bearing, and walk along this, counting the paces until you equal the number of paces used in the first diversion. Finally, revert to your original bearing and resume the walk.

Aiming off

The practice of 'aiming off' is a good one and, a useful tool. Look at Figure 51. You are walking from Point A to Point B. Visibility is poor, and the chance of missing Point B on this stretch of moorland is significant. Only a small error to the left (north) could have you missing the wall altogether. The technique of aiming off avoids the error. Put simply, you take your bearing from Point A to Point B, and

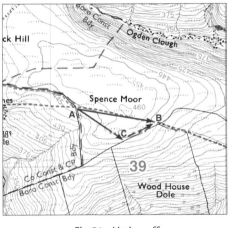

then just walk to the right, i.e. south, of it – in this illustration, towards Point C. Here there is a field boundary – a wall, in fact – and once you reach it, all you have to do is turn left and walk beside the wall until you reach Point B, immediately to the north of a wall junction.

Fig 51: Aiming off

The feature towards which you aim off need not be a wall, of course. It could equally be a stream, river, or the edge of woodland. If you try to hit Point B directly, and miss, you have no way of knowing whether you need to walk left or right to find it. Aiming off ensures that you find your target.

GPS and other technology

Although new technology continues to hit the market at bewildering speed, GPS (Global Positioning System) is here to stay, and has a useful role to play for walkers. It is vital to understand, however, that a GPS is not a substitute for map and compass skills; you need to understand everything that has preceded this chapter before you can properly use a GPS. The Pathfinder® Guide *GPS for Walkers* gives a detailed grounding to GPS and digital maps.

What is GPS?

GPS is a worldwide radio navigation system that uses a network of 24 satellites and receivers to calculate positions. By measuring the time a signal takes to reach the receiver, the distance from the satellite can be estimated. Repeat this with several satellites and the receiver can then use triangulation to establish its position.

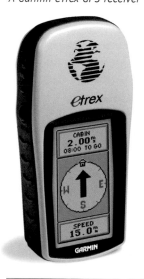

A Garmin eTrex GPS receiver

The receivers used by walkers are small hand-held devices that have a small aerial that picks up the signals. Using geometry, the receiver can work out where you are and, if it can connect with enough satellites, it can also work out how high you are. For the system to work, however, it follows that your hand-held device must have a clear view of the sky. Generally this is not a problem, but prolonged periods in dense woodland can cause the signal to drop.

What can a GPS device do?

Fundamentally, a GPS receiver can tell you where you are, and how high you are. This information can be presented in different ways because you determine the units of measurement you prefer – grid references, latitude and longitude, metres, feet, etc.

The GPS can be used to record information about the route you are walking. This is useful for a couple of reasons:

1. If you need to backtrack to your starting point, you can put the GPS 'in reverse', and it will guide you back the way you came.

2. If you have the appropriate software, you can download the trail you have followed so that it overlays Ordnance Survey mapping, to give a reasonably accurate track of your route.

The facility to pre-store a planned route is quite useful, e.g. using grid references, and then use the GPS to guide you along the route – of course, the GPS does not know about the condition of the terrain and it may link two grid references by a route it is impossible to follow. So, this aspect of the GPS system needs treating with a measure of caution.

At any stage in a walk, you can 'mark' your position, and the GPS will store this. If, later, you need to return to any particular position, the GPS can guide you to it.

How accurate is it?

Accuracy depends on the number of satellites the receiver can 'see'. But experience has shown that the best accuracy the receiver itself will admit to is around 4-5 metres. This, for walking purpose, is good enough in all but the most critical situations, e.g. on a knife-edge ridge. If you then want to impose the details of a route onto Ordnance Survey mapping, then in places the route will not appear to correspond to the mapped route you followed. This is because Ordnance Survey maps use different models for the earth and co-ordinate systems. So, when you try to relate your GPS position to features on the map, the two will differ slightly. The same holds true for elevation, as again different models are used. It is an historical thing, and may be resolved in time, but for the moment you just need to be aware of the issue.

Are there any other problems?

There are a couple of issues. The first is that the hand-held device is battery operated, and even with long-life batteries, it will run out at some stage. So you have to carry spare batteries in your rucksack, and be attentive to the battery condition of your receiver at all times.

The second point has already been touched on: you need to be able to 'see' the satellites, but woodland, high cliffs, caves, all prevent this. Once the GPS loses its signal it can no longer track and record your route. When you 'reappear' it continues, but the trail displayed on the hand-held receiver has breaks in it, and if you download the track to a computer then the route for this blind stretch is shown as a straight line joining the last and next known readings.

Hand-held receivers work best when held horizontally, and will not update until you physically move. It is possible to store a receiver in a jacket pocket and for it to successfully record a route, but better results are obtained if it is held externally.

Is a GPS receiver for you?

Not as a substitute for a map and compass, but it is useful in plotting your position – which you can then check on the map. This is especially helpful in moorland terrain, and even in farmland where rights of way continue to exist but now run along the course of removed field boundaries. Finding the correct line for a footpath can be difficult in these circumstances, but a GPS reading will help plot your position in relation to where you want to be.

If you use one, be sure not to let it take over. Your map and compass are essential – a GPS receiver is not, but it can be an enhancement.

The new kids on the block

Technology never stands still, and already a new breed of GPS is available. The purpose-built, rugged Satmap Active 10 receiver is designed for use with information-rich maps to give outdoor sports enthusiasts the first really useful and reliable, hand-held, integrated GPS and map system which pinpoints precise location on high quality Ordnance Survey mapping. The device also tracks where users have been, logs statistics, and can provide audio-visual points of interest.

First available in May 2007, the Satmap Active 10 comes with free high-quality national road mapping pre-loaded as standard. Own-brand maps for walking and cycling, created using Ordnance Survey data, are available either on SD Cards or sold via Internet downloads.

Only a short way ahead there will be a portfolio of feature-rich maps to cover trails and event maps, such as the Yorkshire Three Peaks race and The Ten Tors, as well as introducing mapping for other European countries. Already available are all the UK National Parks, national trails, ten regional maps, and 67 county maps covering areas such as the Peak District, the Lake District, Dartmoor and the Scottish Highlands.

In the end

Regardless of the usefulness and versatility of modern technology, it has to be powered somehow. It could be disastrous to be relying on a GPS system all day only to find that at the end of the day power fails. Use GPS systems as an add-on to the knowledge you have gained from this book, but never, never, never go without a map and compass.

Altimeters

An altimeter provides a check on location by giving your height. If the altimeter reads 357 metres, then you must be near a 350 metre contour on the map. Tie this in with other information – are you on a descending ridge, for example – and you can fix your position with a fair degree of accuracy. Altimeters tend to be less fashionable than GPS systems, mainly because the GPS gives you more for your money. The position of a GPS satellite never varies, but most altimeters rely on variations in air pressure that occur as height is gained. Moreover, because changing weather patterns influence air pressure, to maintain accuracy an altimeter needs to be reset frequently, whenever you reach a point of known height, e.g. a trig pillar.

Digital mapping

In addition to the sort of mapping that is available on GPS devices, it is now possible to acquire whole sets of maps on CD-ROMs. You can use these on screen to plot routes, add waypoints and generally get a detailed overview of the region you are heading for. Some of the software that is available also allows you to generate a 3-D map so that you can actually see the landscape in much more detail. Digital mapping is becoming increasingly sophisticated, and will play an important role in the future of walk planning and exploration.

Mobile phones

Carrying a mobile phone can be very useful in an emergency.

Bibliography and further reading

Hill, H. *Freedom to Roam* (Moorland Publishing, 1980)

Jarvis, Robin. *Romantic Writing and Pedestrian Travel* (Macmillan, 1997)

Marples, Morris. *Shank's Pony: A Study of Walking* (J M Dent and Sons, London, 1959)

Owen, T and Pilbeam, E, *Ordnance Survey: Map Makers to Britain since 1791* (Ordnance Survey, Southampton, 1992)

Riddall, John and Trevelyan, John. *Rights of Way: A Guide to law and practice* (Open Spaces Society and Ramblers' Association, 3rd ed., 2001)

Salveson, P, *Will yo' Come o' Sunday Mornin'?* (Red Rose Publishing, 1982, republished in 1996)

Shoard, Marion. *A Right to Roam* (Oxford University Press, 1999)

Solnit, Rebecca. *Wanderlust: A History of Walking* (Verso, 2001)

Taplin, Kim. *The English Path* (Perry Green Press, 2nd ed., 2000)

Thomas, Clive. *GPS for Walkers* (Crimson Publishing, 4th ed., 2007)

Index